Boundaries for Empaths

Proven Ways to Establish Personal Boundaries as an Empath or Highly Sensitive Person - Say No Without Feeling Guilty

Amber Wise

Table of Contents

Empath

How to Develop Your Gift and Protect Yourself - A Simple Guide for Highly Sensitive People

Introduction

An empath is a highly sensitive person, one with the ability to feel and experience other people's feelings to a high degree. It is like having an extra sense or perception, which allows the empath to detect feelings, whether positive or negative, from others. Since empaths have the ability to understand whatever is happening around them in their environment, they become especially aware of the emotions of those around them. The empath can pick up others' feelings even if they are not emitting any body language or facial expressions. It is like being able to read a person's mind but through feelings and emotions.

Emotions are essentially energies that an empath picks up on, just as one might pick up on radio waves or electrical currents. Since empaths can pick up on other people's feelings, it is essential they protect themselves from the overwhelming amount of energies they perceive. They are like sponges that soak up other people's energies, and in order to protect themselves from being overcharged, they must learn how to shield themselves. However, just because they are able to sense what is happening around them, it does not necessarily mean they have a desire to interact with people? In fact, most empaths would prefer others to leave them alone.

A person can be an empath even if they are not a naturally sensitive person. However, the more a person can sense other people's energies, the more freedom they have to interact with others and still come out with no internal damage. Empaths who are also sensitive persons often end up absorbing the energy of others to make up for some deficit in themselves. A sensitive person is one who is unable to sense their own emotions and feelings.

Since empaths are easily affected by other people's energies, they have a difficult time in relationships. This is because they take on something of the personalities of those they interact with. This can be good if the person with whom they interact is positive, but it can be devastating if the person is negative. In either case, an empath will tend to take on qualities from others that are not characteristic for them.

For example, I have known women who are very shy and do not like going out. Each time they go out with a negative friend, they end up coming home and complaining about how their friend would not shut up. In this example, the empath is able to sense the negative energy of their friend and then changes into someone more outgoing because this is what their friend seems to be.

Empaths are extremely humble people who do not believe they can do anything special. They feel as though their gift is a curse rather than a blessing. However, empathy is not an ability to be ignored; rather; it is one that should be nurtured and cultivated so the empath can grow into his or her own person with their own unique gift for the great benefit of all in the world.

Those who choose to ignore their empath-ness and not develop their sensitivity will continue to live in a world, where they cannot understand what others are thinking and feeling. They will have to live in a world of strangers.

An empath may have had experiences, where they take on the feelings of others and sense they are not feeling as they normally feel. In this case, the empath will feel lost or confused, not knowing how he or she is supposed to be feeling. At other times, the empath may feel overwhelmed to the point of exhaustion by what seems to be his or her own feelings, such as depression, anxiety and even physical symptoms.

Empaths usually work in careers where they can help others, such as doctors and caregivers. They also excel in artistic careers where they can express their feelings and emotions through their music, art or writing. Many empaths are artists.

An empath can end up harming themselves because of the effects that others have on them. In extreme cases an empath can become a doormat for others, lose their own sense of identity, and become very confused about who they are. Empaths are often accused of having multiple personalities because they change so drastically around different people. They simply take on the energy and qualities of those with whom they interact, whether positive or negative.

The best way to deal with such changes is to determine what causes the empath to change into different personalities and then learn how to shield themselves from those qualities so their own personalities will dominate.

Empaths are always seeking to understand what is happening in the world around them, even if they do not realize what they are doing. They simply want to know why others are the way they are. They want to know what makes other people think, and they simply cannot stand being in the dark about anything. Due to their curiosity about everything around them, they often read a great deal and may become students in their chosen field (whatever it may be) to find answers to their questions.

They are also very intuitive with great curiosity. Being sensitive to energy, they are often able to discern if someone is being truthful or not. As a result, they have the tendency to be attracted to the same type of people over and over again. They end up working with these people or being married to the , only to find that their intuition was correct: they were not the type of people they wanted in their lives.

Again, it is necessary for the empath to learn how to shield themselves from negative energy so they will not take on other people's feelings and emotions. They must learn how to nurture their own gifts instead of allowing them to overwhelm them.

Chapter 1:
What is an Empath?

E mpathy is a gift, as established, and being able to reach out, touch someone, and make a connection is a great way to use it. The background of the empath will be explored before any suggestions are given on how to develop the gift further.

Empaths feel what others feel. This can be interpreted as a curse, but actually it can be quite a blessing to be able to tell how others are feeling and to even understand a little bit of why they felt that way.

There are many different types of empaths based on what they can feel, how it affects them, and what experiences they draw from. Being able to read emotions is one thing, but it means nothing at all if the empath is able to put themselves in other people's shoes. This is a skill that most people have to learn over time as they grow and develop. If an empath is able to use that skill, it can be quite a valuable one.

Some empaths can feel future events as well as emotions. This may sound like an amazing gift, but it can be hard on the empath because they must accept that they cannot change the future. In addition to these more powerful types of empaths, there are those who are just really good at reading and understanding the emotions of others and figuring out what is going on in their lives.

Emotional Energies

Being able to empathize with others' thoughts is not something all empaths can do. It is not that this skill should be ignored if an empath cannot do it, but this is an ability that more people have than they realize. Everyone experiences what they feel and sometimes people give off more energy when they are feeling really strongly about something. The empath is able to pick this up and knows how the other person feels. Most of the time this is just a clue to how they are feeling, but sometimes it will be clearer because the empath is picking up on even more than basic emotions. An empath will feel what others are feeling, and that can be a bit overwhelming if they cannot separate from a person or surround themselves with others less intense.

Emotionally Sensitive

Some people are just more sensitive to what others are feeling because they are naturally this way or may have had experiences where they felt the emotions of others and learned how to handle it.

An empath will feel the emotions of others, but they will not necessarily feel the deeper meaning behind them. The empath might pick up on what the other person is feeling and that is all that they can interpret. This is great for a person who is sensitive, but if they have gone through some type of training, it could be great to know what someone else is feeling.

Empathy in Relationships

When an empath is in a relationship, it can be a bit hard to handle. They can become emotionally involved with someone very quickly. This may seem good at first, but many empaths get hurt. The empath will feel they are being used, which can destroy the trust between them and their partner. It is important for the empath to know that they are not using someone else but have just picked up on the emotions of another and are able to give them what they need. Making a real connection with a person will be much easier if both people understand each other.

In the Workplace

Some people have jobs where they deal with emotions often. A therapist who works with individuals suffering from depression or anxiety will use this skill to help them. The empath is able to feel what the other person is feeling and can understand even if they do not know the reason. It will also be easier for them to deal with people on a day-to-day basis when they are getting all of their emotions from others.

In many cases, the empath knows that something is wrong before the person even realizes it. Even if they cannot do anything about it, the empath will have a better understanding of what is going on, and it will be much easier to deal with the emotions of others.

Turning the Power Off

Some people do not want to feel what others are feeling and that means they will have to learn how to turn off this skill. When the empath picks up the emotions of others, it can be very unpredictable. It depends on who they are with and what they are doing. Sometimes the empath will become overwhelmed by emotions that can be hard on them. If they do not understand why they are having these feelings, it can cause them more stress than they need to have in their life.

Another thing that an empath will need to learn is how not to feel the emotions of others. It sounds a bit strange, but this is an ability they need to function throughout the day. They will feel the emotions of those around them and realize that it is causing them stress. It can be hard to relax until they can make those feelings go away.

Emotional Needs

The empath needs to understand their own emotional needs in order to understand what they need from others. The empath is going to be more sensitive to the emotions of others, but they are also going to understand what they feel and why. This can help them relax. They will also have a good sense of when someone else is not feeling well mentally. It may seem strange, but it is just another part of the empath's ability.

The empath will never be able to completely shut off their empathic skills because they are so natural to use. It is something they have been able to do for their whole life, and it is what makes them who they are. It does not mean there won't be in situations where the empath feels overwhelmed by their emotions, but this can be avoided with some work on their part. Empaths need to learn how to control these feelings and know that they are not feeling what others feel, but only feeling their emotions.

Notes

_____

_____

_____

_____

_____

_____

_____

_____

_____

_____

Chapter 2:
Are you an Empath?
Self-assessment Test

An individual who can sense the emotions of others and is deeply connected to others on an emotional level is an empath. There are four basic types. This test will help you determine how much of an empath you are. There's no right or wrong answers, just answers that feel right for you. Please be as honest with yourself as possible when answering these questions.

- When someone has a great sense of humor, I laugh and enjoy myself.
- When people share their sorrows and joys with me, it helps me to feel connected to them.
- When people touch me affectionately, I can feel the emotion behind it.
- I notice different kinds of energy around me in people, places, and things.
- I pick up on other peoples' moods or emotional states quickly.
- People's emotions affect me in many ways. They can trigger memories of other times I have felt similar emotions.
- I feel as though I am aware of things other people are not.
- I feel emotions other people are feeling.

- My sense of others' emotions is stronger than most people.
- It is easy for me to sense when someone is angry, even if they are trying to hide it.
- When I meet new people, I learn about them by sensing who they are energetically.
- I have a strong intuition about people.
- I know when someone is lying to me, even if they are trying to hide it.
- I can sense positive or negative energy around places or things.
- When I talk with certain people, I know that they are not being truthful.
- When I am with someone who is sad, I feel their sadness more than others might.
- I have visions and dreams of things that happen before they actually do.
- People sometimes tell me my dreams are very real to them as well.
- I feel things more strongly than others.
- Other people's moods or emotions affect me deeply.
- When I am in nature, I experience a sense of calmness and harmony.

- I am deeply moved by beautiful or dramatic events in movies, books, plays, etc.
- I can sometimes tell when people are lying to me.
- People's energy affects me in many ways. I feel very happy or peaceful around some people.
- The moods of the people I am with affect my own moods a great deal.
- When someone touches me affectionately, it makes me feel closer to them.
- It makes a big difference in my day when I am able to interact with nature.
- I notice how beautiful or dramatic everything seems around me and it moves my emotions deeply.
- I notice other people's moods and feelings.
- I often read people's energy, intentions and emotional states.
- I notice things in the environment around me that others don't seem to see.
- It affects my emotions when I am in nature.
- The feelings of others are sometimes like a punch to the gut because I feel them so deeply.

- When I am outside, I can sense the subtle changes in the weather before anyone else does.
- I can sense when someone is trying to hide their true feeling from me.
- I feel a good deal of empathy for others.
- I am very connected to nature and animals.
- When I read, watch movies or TV shows, or go to plays, I notice other people's energies and emotions around me.
- Even when someone is trying to hide their true feelings from me, I can usually tell that they are not being honest.
- I feel strongly when viewing photographs of beautiful scenery or nature.
- Other people's moods or emotions affect me strongly.
- I am emotionally sensitive.
- When I am in nature, I feel very peaceful and happy.
- I am drawn to beautiful places where I feel at peace.
- Other people's moods and emotions affect me deeply.

- When I encounter a situation that is extremely tragic or dramatic, it touches my heart deeply. It makes me cry. Sometimes I connect with something on such a deep level that it feels like my soul is being moved by it. Other times, the sadness can be so overwhelming that it makes me physically ill.
- I have an intuitive sense of things.
- I am sensitive to people's energies.
- I am very sensitive to the moods and feelings of other people.
- It makes a big difference in my day when I get a chance to interact with nature. I feel happier and more energized when I do.
- I am drawn to beautiful scenery, whether it mountains, ocean, woods or gardens. There is also an emotional connection there for me.
- I enjoy being in nature where I feel a sense of calmness and peace.
- I get emotionally touched by music, plays, books and poetry. It makes me feel deeply about things.
- Even when someone is trying to hide their true feelings from me, I know that they are not being

honest. I remain calm during tense or emotional situations because my intuition and gut feelings tell me that all is not as it seems.

- The moods of the people around me affect my own moods a great deal.
- I am strongly affected by the moods, emotions and energies of other people.

- I have visions and dreams of things that are coming to pass in the future.
- I have so much empathy and compassion for others that I often find myself crying from a feeling of loss, sadness or distress.
- I feel very happy or peaceful around some people. Their energies affect me in many ways.
- I am drawn to beautiful things that bring me pleasure. Beautiful music, films, books and art touch me deeply.
- When I am outside during good weather, it makes a big difference in my day because it affects my mood and energy levels in a positive way.

- I love to go to museums, art galleries, science centers and other places where I can view and experience beautiful things.
- When I walk in nature, it makes me feel happy and peaceful. It will also make a great difference in my day when I get a chance to interact with nature. It affects my moods and energy levels in a positive way.
- The music that I enjoy brings me feelings of peace and happiness.
- I enjoy going to plays, concerts or other artistic performances because it lifts me up emotionally. Even if the performance is not that good, I still find myself being deeply affected by it.
- I enjoy being in beautiful natural settings because I feel so happy and peaceful there. The beauty of nature can really move me emotionally; sometimes it can even bring me to tears.
- The moods of the people around me strongly affect my own moods of happiness or sadness.
- I get very emotional when I think about certain things. I can cry or be very moved by a movie, TV

show, book, poem or something else that is beautiful or tragic.

- I am strongly affected by the weather. If the weather is dark and gloomy, it affects me in a negative way. It can really bring me down if I am outside during dark rain or stormy weather.
- I feel like I have a lot of emotional depth. I don't know if everyone feels as deeply as I do, but it seems like most people don't.
- I can get so emotional in certain situations that it gets overwhelming for me.
- When the weather is beautiful, or when the light is soft and warm, I find myself feeling a lot happier than usual.
- I get upset if I can't make myself cry at a sad movie or TV show, or if I can't feel deeply from something that is really beautiful. If I can't cry or feel emotional from something like that, then it's not very good.
- I often feel emotions so deeply that it affects the way I think and act in certain situations. When I am deeply touched by something, my mind can be clouded by these bad emotions and I can even lose

control of my own thoughts. This can lead to me saying or doing really hurtful things.

If "yes" is your answer to most of these questions, then you may be a Highly Sensitive Person. It's not a disorder, and it's not something to fix or get rid of. Being a HSP is what makes you, and there is nothing wrong with that!

What can I do about it?

First, just knowing about the trait can help out a lot. Accepting that you are someone who has a higher sensitivity to your environment is an important step, especially if you have been struggling for years with the feeling of being wrong or weird.

The second thing I would recommend is starting a daily mindfulness practice, which can help you slow down and experience the present moment without being overwhelmed by your environment. Maybe you're familiar with the term "mindfulness" from the many articles out there about how it can help people with depression, stress or anxiety. Mindfulness isn't just for that, however. It can also be helpful if you find yourself feeling emotionally overwhelmed in your daily life.

The basic idea of mindfulness is simply being more aware and present in your life. There are many ways to do this, but there are also many ways that mindfulness might not work for you. What I've learned lately is that we are all different, and what works for one person might not work for another. I have always been a mindful person, and I have found most things (including meditation) to be very helpful. However, the longer I do it, the more aware I am of which activities bring me greater ease and peace of mind.

There are some activities that seem to make things worse, even if they help other people out a lot. I have a friend who tried meditation for a while, but it never seemed to help. She tried many different forms but still could not feel like it was worth her time. Eventually, she gave up. For some people, mindfulness might really help them feel less stressed and overwhelmed in their lives. For others, it might not be helpful at all (or even make things worse). The important thing is to keep trying different things until you find what works for you.

Notes

Chapter 3:
Common Traits of the Empath

T he traits of the empath are many and varied and not always easy to live with, which is why a brilliant empath will always be misunderstood. They are the ones who have to walk on eggshells just to avoid hurting someone's feelings. They are the ones who know that words really do hurt (and heal). They feel what others say, and they "get" what they mean. The little things in life tend to drain them and cause exhaustion because there's so much negativity around them, but they can't get away from it.

Some of their most common traits:

Emotionally Focused People

Empaths are highly sensitive and empathetic to the emotions and feelings of others. Most empaths have trouble tuning into their own emotions because they're picking up on others', or they're living vicariously through another to feel something. In general, empaths are highly empathetic people; they're caring, compassionate and understanding. They have the ability to understand and make deep connections with people. Empaths are incredibly intuitive and can sense when something is wrong. They're often gifted psychic mediums. Sometimes empaths can feel completely drained after spending time around specific people because they pick up on the emotions, negative or positive, of others.

Emotionally unavailable / emotionally distant people

Empaths can identify with emotionally unavailable or distant people because we have felt this way at some point. We struggle to make sense of our feelings. We know what it's like to want something but not be able to figure out exactly what we want. We yearn for something we can't quite put our fingers on. We know what it's like to feel incomplete because we don't "have" whatever is missing.

Emotionally sensitive / Highly Sensitive People

Empaths are highly sensitive people, meaning they're more easily overwhelmed by sensory input, whether noise or smells. They're also tuned into the emotions of others and all the stimuli around them. This can be overwhelming for an empath at times; it can cause them to feel overly emotional or oversensitive. They're also empathetic to the energy of people around them and can often pick up on a good vibe or a bad feeling radiating from someone.

An introvert or an extrovert

Empaths can be introverted or extroverted. They may be shy or outgoing, depending on who they surround themselves with. Empaths are caregivers; they're naturally giving people. They enjoy helping others and being helpful, which is why empaths do well in helping professions like nursing, teaching and counseling.

Empaths are caring and compassionate people but in relationships, they sometimes struggle to set boundaries because they hate letting people down. They're also people pleasers and sometimes let people take advantage of them. Sometimes they can be taken advantage of because there are certain traits they possess that make them easy targets for people who want to take something from them, whether it's their time, energy or attention.

Empaths are emotionally intelligent individuals who have a knack for understanding the emotions of others and responding appropriately. They also sense the bad intentions or dishonesty in others, which is why it's difficult for them to trust people. Empaths don't want to be lied to, and they often avoid being around people who are dishonest.

Empaths are sensitive to others' energies - positive or negative. They go through a psychic shift to better understand how to care for themselves and the people they love.

Empathy is the ability to understand someone's emotional states. An empath is a highly sensitive person, often caring very deeply about others. They're typically quite creative and passionate about the things they love, but get can also be sensitive and fragile. Introverted empaths are quiet and reserved while extroverted empaths are outgoing and expressive.

Emotionally driven people

Empaths are highly emotional beings. They tend to overthink things, and sometimes feel as if they're on an emotional rollercoaster ride. They have mood swings on a dime and sometimes don't even know why. At times, it's difficult for them to make sense of their feelings, but they know we feel things strongly. It's not as if empaths are emotional all day every day; sometimes they're calm, cool, collected and level-headed. But at other times, especially when overexposed to a situation or a person, they become irritable and have emotional breakdowns.

Empaths are always on the go; they're always helping others while putting their needs last. They feel as if they're going through a psychic shift, drained and exhausted from constantly being around people or doing too much. It's important for them to spend time alone to restore themselves.

Empaths pick up on the energy of others, which can be quite overwhelming at times. They want to make sure everyone is happy all the time, and they'll do whatever they can do to achieve this. These very intuitive people have the ability to sense when something is wrong with someone or when a person isn't being honest. They're caring and compassionate but also extremely sensitive, allowing them to feel other people's pain.

Empaths are natural at helping others, but at times this backfires on them. They're sometimes taken advantage of because of certain traits that make them easy targets for inconsiderate people.

Sometimes the Shadow Empath Archetype reveals itself as feeling drained and exhausted. They have the tendency to think over things a lot, and they can seem indecisive. Some days they're emotional and some days they won't let things affect them as much, so it's hard to tell if it's a genuine internal feeling or just an intense feeling of the day.

Emotions are more intense for them than for most people. They feel them more deeply and sometimes have a difficult time letting go. Empaths struggle deeply with all the emotions they feel, and sometimes it feels like there's just too much going on within. They put on a brave face and are often called "peacemakers" because they're always looking for the good in everyone. They don't like to see anyone upset or angry and will do whatever they can to make sure people are happy.

They often feel overwhelmed. Even with just one person, empaths can be affected. Being in an environment with a lot of negative energy can leave them feeling drained and exhausted. If they're in a group of people who are not only feeling negative emotions but also expressing them outwardly, empaths can feel physically ill.

If you're an empath, you know how draining it can be to be around people with negative energy. You know how good is the feeling to be around those who are positive thinkers and genuinely nice people. But being around positive energy doesn't necessarily mean you suddenly don't feel negative emotions anymore. A happy and positive person can still feel negative emotions, but they don't necessarily feel the need to join in or comment on them. If you are around a truly positive person, the best thing you can do is to focus on yourself.

Notes

_____

_____

_____

_____

_____

_____

_____

_____

_____

Chapter 4:
General Types of Empaths

There are many types of empaths. However, this chapter will focus on only the general types. The main thing to remember is that all the empaths listed here are different, just as all non-empaths are different.

Cognitive Empaths

You will find this type of empath in the sciences or other areas where a lot of critical thinking is involved in their work. They are the ones who can debate both sides of an issue logically. However, they are not always able to prevent their emotions from getting involved and often struggle on their own. They end up being the coldest empaths and often associate empaths with people who are weak or over reactive. They are in general not very sociable people unless they need to be at work.

The Cognitive Empath usually has a very good memory and doesn't easily forget what they have learned or read. For that reason, they can give you a lot of information on whatever subject you may ask about. If you want facts this is your type of empath.

Somatic Empaths

Th is the second most common type of empath. These are the ones who feel other people's emotions with their bodies. They can feel a person is ill. You often find these empaths in the medical profession because they can feel another person's pain and want to do something about it. They may be doctors, nurses, or even therapists. They are strong when people need them, but they struggle with sharing too much of themselves with others because they sometimes get drained easily.

The Somatic Empath usually has a hard time focusing on one thing at a time and needs help to ground them. They have a hard time sitting still and need to keep moving or changing tasks. They are natural multitaskers. If you want someone who can fix you, then this is your type of empath.

Emotional Empaths

These are the most common type of empaths. They usually have a hard time not feeling other people's emotions. They have a hard time tuning out people and can become drained easily if they are with people in distress. If you want someone to feel your pain, then this is your type of empath.

Geomantic Empath

These are the rarest of all empaths, but they do exist. They have no idea what it's like to feel emotions; however, they know how other people feel. It is hard for them to tell you what they are feeling because it is like someone else has taken over their bodies and that person feels whatever it is they might be feeling. This person relies on emotions and reactions more than words when trying to understand the people around them.

These empaths don't have many friends because they know of no other way to be. They are stuck in their heads when they try to explain themselves, and people have a hard time understanding them. These empaths are the most likely to be diagnosed with schizophrenia.

The Geomantic Empath usually has a very hard time making decisions and always has an emotional factor involved in what they need to decide about. If you want someone who will not connect with your emotions but will know what you are feeling, then this is your type of empath.

There is no one type of empath and all types have their own gift and struggles. People who are not empaths tend to believe that they have many layers of feeling; it looks to them like they do. However, that is not the case. They have no more layers of feelings, just different layers.

Plant Empath

These are the people who can feel the emotions of plants. This type of empath is in a unique situation where they have to make sure they don't anger a plant or it might die on them. They strive to help plants as much as they can and learn how to care for a plant so it will flourish. All empaths deal with their emotions in different ways and for this type of empath, it is very important not to kill a plant by accident it would be like killing another person's emotions.

Animal Empath

This type of empath can feel the emotions of animals that are like them. They can feel a dog's or cat's emotions about as well as they feel other people's. However, with other animals that are not like them (for example rats) they have a hard time feeling their emotions.

Most empaths tend to have one type of animal they seem to connect with better than others, and they will sense a stronger connection. If you have a cat or other pet that acts like it understands you, then that is probably your type of empath.

The empathic ability has both a passive and an active component. The passive component allows the empath to sense its companion within a twenty-five-foot radius (if the companion is in animal form) or within a mile radius if the companion isn't in animal form.

The companion's condition can be done without giving away the empath's position, as long as the empath remains unobserved. The companion will usually be aware of the empath's presence, however. The active component of the empathic ability allows a level twelve or higher empath to temporarily boost his or her companion's natural abilities. This active ability can only be used once per day for every two levels, so a level twelve or higher empath can use this active ability once per day.

Companions are usually aware of their masters' empathic ability. They may sometimes feel uncomfortable when the empath is using his or her active component to boost abilities, but a level eight or higher empath can solve this problem by temporarily cutting off using this component (usually for one minute). All companions can block communication with other living creatures unless commanded to allow it by their master.

Notes

Chapter 5:
Empath Types

There are a number of different empaths, each with various levels of abilities. For example, there are "high functioning" and "low functioning" empaths. There are also low level and high level empaths. Each type has its own set of gifts, skills and abilities that make it unique from other types within their group.

There is also a special kind of empath often referred to as the "master" or "plus" empath. These are the rarest and most powerful of all the types. Studies have shown that less than 1% of empaths are master types. New studies show a growing number of these empathic master types currently in existence throughout the world today.

A large number of empaths, who are not master types, have long been frustrated by their inability to control their abilities and by the fact that they seem to be adversely affected by others' emotions. Having the ability to turn their abilities off and on, master/plus empaths can tune into another person's emotions at will and control how they respond.

The Low Functioning Empath

Low functioning empaths are those who can't turn their empathic abilities off. They continually have to deal with the stream of emotions flowing into them from other people, which can be very draining.

Many of these low functioning empaths become bitter about having this power and either develop anger issues or withdraw deep inside themselves. These empaths are often misunderstood by normal type people and often teased or bullied for being "too sensitive."

For these reasons, low functioning empaths often grow up to be introverted, shy or withdrawn people who care very deeply about others but can't seem to find the right path in life. They sometimes feel awkward or out of place in a world that is completely foreign to them.

To compensate for their lack of control over their empathic abilities, they have developed the habit of shutting down their emotions to the outside world to protect themselves from the negative influences of other people. They come across as cold and unfeeling to normal types who can sense that something is "off" about these low functioning empaths.

Low Functioning Empaths and their Children

Low functioning empaths often have children who are also empaths because empathy is genetic. Low functioning empaths often feel they must give birth to more and more empaths to survive themselves. The children of low functioning empaths are often forced by society to be "the good child" and sort out all the problems that they sense in their mother or father or they will end up being caught in the middle of a battle between warring parents.

Low Functioning Empaths and their Empathic Abilities

Low functioning empaths are unable to block out the emotions they receive from other people. They can't turn their empathic abilities on and off like the master/plus empath in order to protect themselves from some of these negative influences. This makes it very difficult for them to deal with normal people who are very insensitive, cruel, selfish, manipulative or abusive in any way.

The High Functioning Empath

High functioning empaths have something their low functioning counterparts don't have—the ability to shut off their empathic abilities at will. They can control their empathic senses so they only pick up positive or neutral emotions from other people and not the harsh, negative ones.

High functioning empaths are often very successful in life because they know how to filter out the harshness of others' emotions, problems or negativity; therefore, they don't feel compelled to add their own negative emotions to the mix.

These high functioning empaths have a wide range of positive emotions that they can pull from to help themselves and others become successful in life; they are completely comfortable with "normal" people.

High Functioning Empaths as Teachers

High functioning empaths often find it very easy to teach others about life or business because they can send out positive emotions to their students so they feel like the teacher is really on their side. High functioning empaths often succeed in fields such as counseling, teaching, acting or writing. They are popular and respected by their students because they teach with caring and empathy.

High Functioning Empaths as Parents

High functioning empaths are very successful at parenting. Because they understand emotions so well, they know how to guide their children through the difficult times of childhood into adults who have developed strong emotional skills themselves.

High functioning empaths can be very successful at teaching their children about love, compassion and empathy. High functioning empaths usually have many friends and a wide network of people who respect them because they treat others in a caring way.

High Functioning Empaths as Friends

High functioning empaths are often the best friends you could have. They treat their friends with respect and are often willing to listen to them vent about problems, burdens or other emotions that are weighing on them. They are often the person to call when you need someone to talk to.

High functioning empaths also have very good emotional intelligence and can easily sense what type of emotion someone is feeling at a given moment. They are fascinated by emotions—why they occur, how they feel, how people respond to them and so on.

Because they don't pick up on negative emotions in others, high functioning empaths can be very fun and easygoing people who like to laugh about situations with their friends. They're very interested in the lighter side of life.

High Functioning Empaths as Lovers

High functioning empaths are quite popular with the opposite sex because they give others so much positive attention, love and understanding. They are often the person who will sacrifice their own needs to make sure that others get what they need.

High functioning empaths make very good lovers because they give back to their partners in a way normal types rarely can. They are able to tune into their partner's emotions and give them the love, understanding, support and reassurance they need to feel good about themselves.

When a high functioning empath chooses a partner, they usually choose someone who is gentle with them. They gravitate toward partners who do not criticize, belittle or disrespect them and automatically treat them with love and admiration.

High Functioning Empaths as Leaders

High functioning empaths make excellent leaders. They usually have a good sense of business, compassion, empathy and caring that goes a long way toward motivating their employees to work hard for the company.

High functioning empaths usually have a sense of loyalty to those who work for them. They go out of their way to help their employees solve problems that arise at work and often treat them like family.

High functioning empaths are often great organizers in leadership roles because they use empathy to sense what needs to be done for the whole group or company be together and have fun working together.

The Inattentive Empath

Most empaths are aware that they have an ability to sense people's emotions, but there's one type who isn't: the inattentive empath. The inattentive empath doesn't even realize that he/she has this ability and feels it is normal for them to be quite connected with their friends, family and the world around them.

The inattentive empath easily forms close bonds with people but never quite realizes that it's because of their empathic nature. Their ability to read others' emotions is often dismissed as being intuitive or creative rather than something that a small percentage of the population can do.

The inattentive empath usually does not fit the image of the emotional person who cries at sad movies and gets teary eyed at emotional events, but they are still an empath.

The Insupportable Empath

One empath often dismissed by society and even by other empaths is the insupportable empath. This type of empath feels overwhelmed at times by the feelings of others. They feel like they're drowning in the emotions of those around them, and it can be overwhelming for them to be in a room full people, no matter how close they are to those people.

The insupportable empath will usually avoid parties, crowded areas and emotionally charged events. The feelings of others can be so overpowering that it is all they can do to help the feeling person without losing themselves in the process.

A symptom that can be attributed to the insupportable empath is the feeling of "entering" a room with many people in it. Before going into such a room, they know they will feel everyone's emotions as their own. Some even say they can feel the room before entering it!

The empath will feel others' feelings so intensely that it will be unbearable. They will know what another person is feeling and how they are feeling about themselves, others, and life in general. This empath may even take on the physical symptoms of the person with whom they are interacting.

They usually have a strong sense of knowing without really being able to explain why. They may have the ability to tell you things about yourself that you don't want to reveal.

The insupportable empath will usually try to distract themselves from these feelings by turning off their empathic abilities, but they do this at their own risk. They may become completely unaware of what is going on around them.

In some cases, the insupportable empath has no choice but to be aware of everyone else's feelings all of the time or risk going insane. Sometimes, the only way to deal with such a situation is to leave society behind and withdraw from people completely.

The Self-Actualized Empath

There is one more type who is different from the rest. It is the self-actualized empath. This type of empath has learned not only to deal with their own feelings, but they have also learned to master the ability to tune into others' emotions and love them even when others are being cruel or abusive.

This empath is also known as the healer. They can help another person or even a group of people calm down and find peace in a situation where they are extremely upset about something.

Self-actualized empaths are very grounded individuals who have knowledge how to deal with their own emotions as well as those of others. They know when others need them to step in and understand what someone else is going through without making judgments about it themselves.

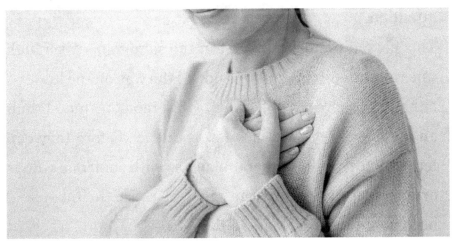

The In-Betweener Empath

The in-betweener is someone in between a high functioning and low functioning empath. Like the high-functioning empath, they possess all the positive attributes that the high-functioning empath has. They also have many of the negative ones too, like being easily drained by others emotions and having a hard time thriving under certain conditions.

When an in-between is with someone, they can feel their energy but not always as strongly as a high functioning empath would. They can sense the emotions of the person but don't have as much of a reaction to them. The in-between empath is able to understand what the other person is feeling and why, but doesn't necessarily resonate with those feelings or need to give them much (if any) attention.

This person's empathy is not in the same range as a high functioning empath, but it is not all the way on the low end either. There are varying levels of difference or "mood" that an in-between empath has to experience before they can feel empathy. If their mood matches with someone who is exuberant, the in-between can feel closer to them and become energized by it. If they are in a more reserved mood, they might get a little irritated by someone who is over-the-top happy.

Notes

Chapter 6:
Benefits, Drawbacks, and Dangers of Empathic Power

E very living being has the capacity for empathy. It is an essential aspect of survival to sense the feelings and emotions of those around you. However, like everything else in life, there are varying levels of ability and intensity. Some individuals are able to pick up and read the feelings of others, even those from thousands of miles away. They can tell when someone is lying or if someone is in pain, even if they aren't present. These individuals are empaths, and they have astonishing control over their abilities. This section will cover benefits, drawbacks, and dangers of empathic power.

Empathic ability is a bit like a radio. There is a dial to tune into various feelings in a range. On low, you can only pick up surface emotions, and it may be difficult to discern what emotion someone is feeling. At mid-range you can get basic feelings such as happiness or sadness. At high-range close to the maximum, you will be reading emotions with complete accuracy and have dialed into the individual's mind.

The benefits of being an empath:

A truly empathic character can sense and feel the emotions of those around him and even gain insight into their thoughts. The more empathic the character, the greater the area he can sense.

If an empath trains himself to sense only negative emotions, he can even become a living lie detector. If he gains enough training in his powers, an empath can also use them to gain information about those around him without being detected.

An empath can establish a powerful rapport with others, easing communication considerably.

The empath is able to understand and predict the actions of people with uncanny accuracy. The empath can also use his powers to influence those around him indirectly. An empath in action is a very intimidating sight - as those who face you can sense the power they provoke in you.

The drawbacks of being an empath:

You must control your reactions to the emotions around you; if you become overwhelmed by emotion, you will be consumed by them lose all understanding and control of yourself.

An empath has no real defenses against an attack that involves the use of emotions - emotions are for an empath like a physical weapon. If you are covered in the emotion of fear, you will take physical damage. Because of the nature of his powers, an empath is at a constant risk that others will find out about them.

If you lose control over your empathic powers, you will be overwhelmed by the emotions around you and lose all understanding and control of yourself.

Usually, a character with empath powers also possesses some kind of secondary ability - if he does, this secondary power is more likely to cause problems than be helpful.

An empathic character cannot "ignore" their power. If he tries to turn it off, it will affect anyone he is in contact with at that time. Also, an empathic character cannot act against the feelings of someone he is in contact with since his mind will be clouded by their emotions, and he won't be able to think straight.

An empath must be careful around those who possess the ability to generate or control emotion - such as telepaths with power over emotions, those with emotional powers, or others with some kind of unusual ability.

If an empath is "forced" to lose his powers, his body will begin to suffer from "emotional shock." An empath must maintain a high degree of control over his emotions to use his powers.

The dangers for an empath:

The danger is in the use of empathic powers. If an empath uses his powers, he risks being overwhelmed by the emotions around him. This can lead to emotional shock, which in turn may lead to death. Because of this danger, empaths are the most feared and respected of all parahumans.

An empath must deal with the fact that people will be aware of his power simply by coming into contact with them. It is easy for an enemy to trigger emotional shock in others simply by attacking them with an emotion the empath can sense.

If you lose control over your empathic powers, you will be overwhelmed by the emotions around you and lose all understanding and control of yourself. This, in turn, may result in the loss of control over your body. The empathic power will take control of your body, and you will be unable to stop it.

An empath is forced to deal with his own emotions as well as the emotions of those around him. A strong empath must train his powers to keep himself from being overwhelmed by them. An empath has little choice but to remain calm, otherwise he risks emotional shock.

The empath must concentrate while in rapport with another character. He must concentrate on the emotions around him to gain insights into the thoughts of those around him - if he is concentrating on anything else, his mind will be clouded and he won't be able to establish rapport.

Because an empath can be dangerous, people will often want to recruit him in their own conflicts against those who might pose a threat. This can lead the empath into situations he would rather avoid.

Note that it is possible for those with mental powers, such as telepaths, to sense the presence of an empath, leading them to believe there are empaths about when there are not.

The empath power is one of the more powerful mental powers in the game, and it can be very dangerous to use. It literally allows someone to feel the emotions of another person; for example, if you are in contact with someone who is afraid, you will feel their fear.

An empath must be wary of those with unusual powers, since they pose a threat to his life, not just his sanity. An empath does not have any real defenses, as being attacked with emotion is tantamount to being attacked with a physical weapon. This means that the empath must rely on dodging, stealth, or allies to survive.

The most dangerous thing for an empath is the loss of control over his powers. Empathic powers are not commonly found. All empathic people suffer from some kind of secondary power. In fact, their empathy is so powerful, it is impossible to ignore or turn off. Companion Powers are used in physical contact with another person. The strength and variety of these abilities depends on the power level of the primary power and whether or not the secondary power is independent or linked to the primary power.

In case you are not familiar with Companion Powers, let me explain how they work. Whenever a primary power is in use, a Companion Power can be selected at the same time. The primary power will affect anyone within range who can feel the Companion Power; it is possible for more than one person to feel the Companion Power from the same source, but only if they are very close and touching each other.

An empath, for example, has the primary power of Empathic Sense. When this power is in use, everyone within his radius (which is 12 yards) that can feel the Companion Power (i.e., Awareness/Empathic Awareness as a secondary power), will be able to sense any emotions nearby - whether or not they are directed at them.

The Empathic Sense companion power is one that can be used to read people's emotions, although the empath will have to concentrate in order to do so. In this case, the primary power is the one that will be used first, followed by a quick switch to the Companion Power in order to read the emotions of those around him.

The stronger the Empathic Sense, the stronger and more accurate the Companion Power will be. The greater number of people who feel this Companion Power from one empath also adds to its strength and accuracy.

Notes

_____

_____

_____

_____

_____

_____

_____

_____

Chapter 7:
Making the Most of it

A person with psychic or emotional powers (empath) possesses a special ability to feel and experience the feelings or emotions of others. Empaths are highly sensitive to the emotional atmospheres of not only others but also places, objects, and animals too. They are able to discern and understand their thoughts. As a result, they are also highly sensitive to the energies of people and things.

Empaths have the ability to feel others feelings, physical pain and symptoms, hear voices, see visions or even know what others are thinking. They can connect with animals too. They will feel restless when an overwhelming presence of a new person is in their environment. They can tell if someone has hostile intentions.

Starting from the time they are babies, empaths can apparently sense the feelings of their parents. They can even sense if a parent isn't feeling well.

Empathies cannot stand extreme anger, fear and pain because these emotional energies affect them badly, and they can get easily drained. Empaths have the ability to focus in situations or places with sudden bursts of intense negative emotion. Some describe this as "getting picked up by the energy" and it can be quite stressful.

Emotional Empaths are often eager to help others, but they are also more inclined to involve themselves in other people's problems. It is very important not to get too involved in the emotions of others.

It is valuable for empaths to understand themselves better, learn how to quiet their minds, practice meditation and develop their intuition. This will help reduce their sensitivities, shielding them from too much noise and thus protecting themselves from getting completely drained.

The following steps can help empaths to make the most of their gift:

Step 1 - Make Friends with Your Sensitivity

Empaths have the ability to feel other's feelings. They also have the ability to hear words and phrases that others say sub-consciously, which is called "thought transference". Empaths will also pick up the emotional energies of others, which can cause them to feel drained. So, making friends with your sensitivity is important.

Emotions will always be there, and you have to learn to deal with them. It is important to understand that how you react emotionally depends on your own personal beliefs, values and how you were raised. Realize that all negative emotions are temporary in life; they will pass and change. Spend time with other empaths and learn how they deal with their sensitivities.

The way you perceive and deal with sensitivity also depends on your personality traits. For instance, highly sensitive people are often shy, introverted and quite. They dislike crowds and large gatherings. Avoidance is common for an empath when they feel uncomfortable in a particular environment or situation, so they have to learn how to avoid what doesn't serve them well.

Step 2 - Balance Your Energy

Negative energies affect the empaths and drain their energy. They have to be aware of the people around them, where they go, how they react and what situations or places trigger strong emotions in them. It is very important for empaths to shield themselves from all negative energies. Empaths should always work on protecting their energies and stay grounded by eating healthy food, exercising regularly and getting enough sleep. They need to stay clear of situations and people that bring too much negativity into their lives.

When empaths experience too many emotions or energies throughout the day, they have to find a way to dissolve the excess energy so they don't feel overwhelmed. A Reiki or EFT session can be very helpful. It is good for them to learn how to ground their energy by connecting with Mother Earth or Father Sun. They can ask for protection from all negative energies around them.

For empaths, it can also be very helpful to wear or carry healing crystals to protect themselves from getting affected by others negative emotions. When in crowds of people, they can use a grounding and protective stone to disconnect.

Step 3 - Do Self-Care

Empaths have the tendency to give too much energy and attention to their loved ones without being aware of it. They need to learn their limits and know when it's time to take a break and have some "me time".

It is important for empaths to develop healthy boundaries. Their friends, family members and loved ones may have taken advantage of them at some point in time. They have the tendency to give too much without expecting anything in return. By learning to set boundaries, empaths protect themselves from getting used or drained by other people.

Empaths must learn how to say "no" when it's needed and to stick with their own decisions. They need to be careful while making friends or accepting help from others, as they may co-create similar relationships in the future.

Step 4 - Take Care of Your Body

Empaths have the tendency to push their bodies past its limits without realizing it. They need to learn to take care of their bodies, thoughts and emotions so they don't get exhausted.

In short, it is important for empaths to monitor their physical and mental health. They should make time for themselves every day to recharge. Regular exercise can help them sleep better at night, as well as be more focused and positive throughout the day.

Empaths need to take care of their nervous system so that they don't get overwhelmed by too many emotions or energies . They should avoid watching the news or anything that can trigger their emotions.

Eating healthy food is also important for empaths since it helps them remain grounded and centered. They should avoid processed food, sugar and caffeine because these substances can make them unfocused.

Finally, empaths need to have a sense of humor about themselves since they are often easily affected by others' thoughts and emotions. If they can't laugh at themselves, they will always feel drained by the world around them.

Step 5 - Be Positive, Patient and Persistent

Empaths are often the people who want to help others with their problems. They have the tendency to fix other people's issues without even realizing it. They need to learn how to be positive, patient and persistent.

When an empath is involved in helping or healing others, they should only do so if it feels right. They should not do this to make themselves feel better or because they think they are helping other people.

One of the main ways for empaths to help others is by applying their own self-healing techniques. When they are feeling drained, they should do something that makes them feel better. They don't have to make other people's troubles feel better since that may end up draining them even more.

Step 6 - Keep Learning

Empaths have a tendency to want to save everyone. They need to keep learning new things to avoid this tendency. One of the empaths' best approaches to learn is by reading self-help literature since they can get a lot of information from other people who have been in their shoes. They may also want to find a mentor who can teach them how to deal with their abilities.

One of the best ways for an empath to learn is by observing other people and situations around them. They need to figure out what is wrong and why a certain situation is the way it is. This can help them avoid draining themselves in the future by shunning similar situations or people.

Step 7 - Work on Boundaries

Empaths need to learn how to set boundaries with others. This can help them have a better image of who they are and what they will tolerate from other people. Empaths may also want to find a good therapist to help them learn how to set boundaries.

Step 8 - Be Honest with Themselves

Empaths need to be honest with themselves. They don't want to avoid the truth since they need to learn about reality and not avoid it. This will help them know what is going on around them and why they are feeling the way they feel in certain situations.

Step 9 - Find a Career

Empaths may want to find the right profession or career that they feel comfortable with. This helps them put their energy into something they are passionate about and have a good time doing it. They will be able to share their talents and gifts with others.

Step 10 - Connect with Nature

Empaths find it easy to connect with nature, since they are so in tune with the world around them. They can connect with nature on an emotional level. When they are feeling stressed or have had a hard day, it can be really healing to spend time in nature. It provides a sanctuary from the chaos of daily life, and lets them renew their energy. The best way to do this is to go outdoors and get some fresh air.

Notes

Chapter 8:
Protecting from Manipulators

There are many different types of people that are almost like villains to empaths. Manipulators, narcissists, energy vampires, psychopaths, and sociopaths are going to be the biggest challengers for an empath.

It is important to remember that at the end of the day, all of these people are just that - people. They have issues of their own to work through. Empaths can help others. It is important for them to know if they should stick around that person or if the relationship is dangerously toxic.

First, you have to identify these people. There are certain qualities that all toxic people hold. If you know someone like this well, you probably already have an idea of what their common qualities are.

Empaths can be these types in some circumstances too. Most empaths internalize their negative energy, but there will still be some who feel such great pain that they do nothing else but express it onto other people.

Exhibiting certain behavior traits isn't a direct indication that you are that type of personality. We all have moments where we might angrily snap, show passive aggression, or even minorly manipulate in an attempt to heal ourselves or at least get a favorable outcome. Anyone like this isn't a terrible person you have to write off, but we still need to be careful when we encounter potentially toxic people.

Energy Vampires

Most people have an image in mind when they hear the word "vampire." It usually involves sharp teeth and some minor to major blood sucking. When we say "energy vampire", we're talking about a metaphorical person who sucks the life out of the people they're around.

An energy vampire takes the positivity from an empath. They'll see that influx of emotion and ability to feel greater and deeper and feed off of it because they don't have much left to feed off.

They will not realize their negative behavior and will instead get to a place where they refuse to change and just try to manipulate other people. Energy vampires have trouble recognizing when they are wrong. They see the world in a dark light, and instead of admitting they might be the problem, they externalize and place blame on others.

To protect yourself from energy vampires, make sure you are setting boundaries with other people. Reflect on the relationship. Ask yourself if it is helping or hurting you overall.

Effects of a Manipulator

When someone manipulates you, whether it is a narcissist or sociopath, it can be very damaging to your abilities as an empath. Manipulators will often do whatever they have to in order to protect themselves. Sometimes, this is a subconscious attempt to heal pain deep within themselves, or it might be a more surface-level conscious attempt to simply get what they want.

A manipulator can make you very confused, causing it to be challenging to trust your own thoughts. There might even be a level of dependency on the manipulator. They might break you down to a point where you don't trust yourself, and instead you only want to believe what they have to say. When someone has hurt you as an empath, it becomes hard to know if anything you think in the future is right.

Red Flags

There are common red flags to be aware of when it comes to manipulators and energy vampires. Some manipulators will play the victim. They make sure that you know if you've hurt them but will never listen when you try to express how they might have hurt you.

They might try and convince you that you are crazy, or what you are feeling isn't validated. They'll tell you that you're "too emotional," as if that were a bad thing. They will make you feel as though your emotions are inconveniencing them.

Manipulators, especially narcissists, have the need to control others. This often comes from a great desire within themselves to have control over their surroundings.

They will not admit that they are wrong and will, instead, go as far as lie to make sure they are right. They will by hypocritical, often having a double standard. As an empath, when you start to sense these qualities in others, it's time to question if you have the energy to work through that relationship and help them or if you would both be better off apart.

Knowing When to Help or Leave

There's a fine line between knowing whether you should help someone or let them figure things out on their own. Remember that no one is going to change unless they are willing and actively trying to change.

There are some things that people just have to learn on their own. As much as you might wish to help them, you have to let them figure out certain things on their own.

This can be very challenging for an empath. If you feel like you are losing yourself in the process, you have to question if it is worth helping them. Some people will become dependent on you, so you have to be wary of this happening.

Healing Yourself First

You are not going to be able to fully help someone else unless you are taking care of yourself first. Sometimes, you might go through the healing process with another person; it can be very helpful to go through something challenging with another person.

Always remember that you should not be putting too much of yourself on the line for someone who wouldn't do the same if they could. Sometimes, there are going to be relationships more weighted in a certain direction. You have to ask yourself if they are willing to pick up the slack, or if they have in the past.

Codependency

Codependency is often misunderstood. It involves a need to take care of someone. There are people out there who need help and can't do it on their own. It is completely fine to help someone else. This kind of care becomes dangerous when it is classified as codependent. Codependency isn't being dependent on another person but being dependent on the need to care for that other person.

Make sure you ask yourself what you are getting out of the relationship. If you feel as though taking care of them is fulfilling part of you, ensure that it is not codependency.

Chapter 9:
Finding Empathic Joy

E mpathy describes the ability to relate and feel with another living being. Empathy flow from sympathy, so they are related. A person with profound sympathy can connect to others' feelings and emotions. Empathy has so many benefits; it helps you appreciate the environment around you, enriching the quality of your life.

You can learn how to live a meaningful life by trying some of these tips:

- Develop your relationships and connection with family members and friends.
- Develop your connection with yourself.
- Spend time away from the television and your computer and spend more time living in the present.
- Focus on gratitude; keep a journal of three things you are grateful for every day.
- Always be aware or mindful for your surroundings; be aware of the needs of others.

Empathy is an important tool for developing stronger relationships and living a more meaningful life. By using empathy, you can find joy in life. Empathy is a form of understanding other people's lives and feelings. It helps to build rapport with others. Empathy is very important in developing a deep relationship with others.

There are several ways how you can develop empathy:

- Learn to be empathic. You need to become aware of what someone else is going through and understand the feelings they are experiencing.
- Be responsive; show your appreciation when someone shares their deepest feelings and try to offer them support and guidance.

Empathy can help you build rapport and trust. This will make a huge impact on your relationships and how you live your life. You may be empathic with others but do you know how to be empathic for yourself? Being empathic for yourself is very important because so many of us have lived by the "give, give, give" motto. We give to others, but we don't stop to think about what we need.

To be empathic for yourself, you need to stop and think about what makes you happy. Think about what makes fulfilled and satisfied with your life. Make sure that your actions are based on self-empathy; if you do something that does not make you happy, it's not worth the time doing it.

- Clean out your closet and donate the unused stuff you no longer need.
- Don't watch television for a whole day; instead, go out and do things you have wanted to do for a long time.
- Spend a morning reading a book or taking a walk; do the things you want to do instead of being stuck inside all day.
- Think about ways you can make your life more meaningful and fulfilling.

It is important to enjoy your gift of empathy. You are given this gift to make your life more meaningful and fulfilling. Not all people have the ability to feel empathy. Empathy has helped me make my life more enjoyable and happy.

Empathy allows people to relate and understand emotions present in others. It is an important skill that helps you to feel connected with the world around you. Understanding the feelings of others leads to deeper relationships and many new experiences in life. You need to use empathy as a way of understanding what someone else is going through, without feeling sorry for them or putting your feelings on top of theirs. Sometimes, people cannot help but feel empathy because they don't know how to avoid it.

Empathy is very useful in one-to-one relationships. In my opinion, the most valuable quality of empathy is its ability to develop strong emotional connections with another person and to feel joy for others.

The relationship between empathy and joy is interesting. When you work on your sense of empathy, you can find joy in life and in other people's lives as well. It helps you to connect with others' feelings. Empathy is a powerful force that allows you to understand and appreciate someone else. People with depth of empathy can connect to others' feelings and share in their joy.

Empathy plays a key role in connecting with other people's feelings. When you feel empathy, it means you enjoy watching another person's life. That is why when someone is live an interesting life or feeling happy, if you are empathic, then you will experience happiness with them. Empathic joy is a great way to connect to the present moment and appreciate what is happening in your life.

There are so many things you can do to feel empathic joy. The first is to live in a present moment. The more you are able to focus on the present moment, the easier it is to enjoy life now. Another great way to feel empathic joy is by noticing it in your daily life. It will not be hard because when you are looking at things around you, they are so interesting and meaningful. Finally, you can feel empathic joy by doing something nice for others. Many people need help and support. You can choose to do something nice for them, and it will feel really good. When you sense the joy you bring to others, that is empathic joy.

Chapter 10:
Loving an Empath

If you have a relationship with an empath, you know it is truly a unique experience. If you are not in a relationship with one, or have not yet developed a close enough bond to know this, then let me enlighten you.

To start off, an empath is a person who feels everything on such an incredible level that they experience life very differently than the average person. You might ask yourself how this could even be possible. They feel everything, including your bad moods, your negative emotions, and even the emotions of others.

It is almost as if they take your negative emotions upon themselves. This is because empaths have what is known as "thin skin." This means they are very sensitive to what is happening around them, and in essence, take all of these feelings into themselves. Empaths are not just people who feel things intensely; they actually feel things not even happening to them at all, and may even happen to other people!

In relationship with You

Empaths have a very hard time dealing with negative feelings or any type of hardship. In fact, they are emphatic about the feelings of others, and this is also why they love being around happy people. They thrive on positive energy and want nothing but the best when it comes to their relationships.

The big problem for empaths is that their feelings are so intense that they have a hard time putting up with the negativity of others. They have to be with people who are happy, upbeat and positive to feel happy themselves.

If you are in a relationship with an empath, or even if you simply interact with one on a regular basis, there are some things you should know. For starters, they feel things very deeply. They care a great deal about what you have to say. They want to listen and relate to you on a deeper level. It is their way of showing that they really do care and how much they love being around you!

They want to make others happy – another way for empaths to show how much they love being with you. Because of their ability to feel the emotions of others, they want nothing but the best for those around them. They want to make you happy and make everyone else around happy as well.

Empaths are highly intuitive – in fact, they pick up on things that most people do not. They sense emotions and things about a person that others may not even notice. This is why they can sometimes seem a bit psychic. They are just very in tune with the world around them, which makes it hard for them to be around negative energy because it would offend their very nature.

An empath is easy to fall in love with, but it may come with a few complications. As much as they love everyone around them, sometimes you just have to pull away or take a break before things get out of hand.

Raising an Empath

If you are the parent of an empath, it is important to understand how your child might be different. They may need more time to themselves, and they might even appear a bit shy at times. This is because they are sensitive to many things in their environment, which can make them a bit cautious. It does take a great deal of time for them to get used to a new place or situation before they feel comfortable with it.

One thing that empaths tend to do well in social situations is listening. They pay attention to what people think and how they feel. This is why they can relate so well to those around them. They like being a good listener, and this is how they show their love. They want to support others in any way they can and to make sure that everyone is happy and comfortable.

An empath truly thrives on positive energy, so be wary of your negative feelings towards others when you are around them. Remember that they take on the emotions of people around them, which means if you are upset about something, odds are they will be upset as well.

This may make them appear overly emotional to others. However, this is simply their way of showing that they feel what you feel. They are not trying to be dramatic; they simply can't help it!

They care about you and want to make sure you are happy. This is why it is important to show your appreciation for everything that an empath does for you. They will feel appreciated and loved by those around them, which is the most important thing of all!

Being a Friend

Whether you are friends with an empath or in a relationship with one, it is important to understand that they care about you and want the best for you. If they seem overly interested in what you have to say, it is probably because they take things so deeply that they actually care about the outcome of what is happening around them.

It is important that if you are friends with an empath, you do not disregard everything they say as being dramatic.

95

They are simply putting themselves in your shoes and feeling what you feel. This is something they cannot always control, which can leave you feeling weird at times.

People who are friends with empaths may feel as though there is too much pressure to be happy and not think about anything negative. If you feel this way, it is important to understand that an empath will only be as happy as the people around them. If your emotions are negative, then theirs are as well.

If you feel as though they are becoming too upset about something that is not even their fault, take a break from each other so that they can calm down on their own.

Notes

_____

_____

_____

_____

_____

_____

_____

Chapter 11:
The Empath and Energy Vampires

E mpaths are in tune with the energies of others and are very low on the list of targets for energy vampires. An empath will see through a vampire's game immediately and almost all empaths scoff at the idea that they could be used by them. There are two reasons an empath is not an easy target: one, they know what kind of human treats people as a means to an end; and two, they sense right away when another person is trying to manipulate them with their feelings. So, empaths are less likely to be manipulated by a vampire; and if they are, the empath will know right away that something is wrong.

There is that saying: be careful what you wish for. In this case, it is best not to wish for too much sensitivity when you are an empath or psychic. The downside of being overly sensitive is that it leaves you open to manipulation by energy vampires.

What is an Energy Vampire?

There are those who take the energy from others. They do not necessarily do this consciously. This is not to be confused with those people who take energy but give back in return, which all healthy relationships require to some degree. The most common expression of an energy vampire is that they try to manipulate others by offering their help or caring to get what they need in return, which is often a feeling of being needed and loved.

Here are some common examples of this behavior:

- A parent wheedles and manipulates their child into babysitting for them.
- When a person becomes overly friendly with you when they see that you will do something for them, such as give them a ride to the airport if they buy you lunch or make cookies. This kind of friendliness is usually seen in people who are lonely.
- When your neighbor who always watches your mailbox for you, asks you to keep an eye on her house when she goes out of town and then phones you every day "to let me know if anything is wrong."
- When a person constantly tells you about other people's problems but does not want to hear about yours.
- If someone gives to you but expects more in return, such as: buying gifts or lending money for ulterior motives.

The danger of energy vampires is that they steal your life force, and energy and make you feel drained or unhappy. When you are in a situation where someone is taking from you and giving nothing back, it can be very confusing because most human beings naturally want to give to others—this is not a bad thing. If you're dealing with an emotional vampire, however, you will need to deal with these feelings of confusion and perhaps even guilt to regain your balance.

Here is how to get your energy back from an emotional vampire:

- Cleansing yourself: give all thoughts and feelings over the situation to God. Ask for help to find the right words and behavior to stop the energy drain so you can go on with your life.
- Laugh about it. Sometimes when we are overly empathic, we start taking everything personally—even jokes and remarks not intended to hurt us. Before you react to something someone has said or done, make sure you are not taking it too personally.

- If someone does not understand why you have backed away from them, tell them, "I need more energy for myself."
- If you become aware of a pattern in your life, it is wise to examine your own behavior. It may be that you are taking too much from others.

Some people are naturally more empathic than others, and this can make them targets for energy vampires. A person with an overabundance of empathy is sometimes referred to as an empath. Empaths often feel the emotions of those around them. While this can be a wonderful gift, it has a downside. Empaths take the emotions of others into themselves—especially when dealing with people with negative emotions. This can leave an empath feeling drained and unhappy.

Notes

Chapter 12:
Strategies for Alleviating Mental and Emotional Distress

On the whole and not just for empaths life is tough. People are hurting out there. As an empath, it is so easy to assume that you are the only one undergoing emotional pain. But always realize that most people are in a world of pain. In our day-to-day living, we run into various things that make our lives difficult. Instead of giving up, we should learn about new tricks to improve the quality of our lives.

The life of an empath is marked by emotional volatility. For an empath to lead a normal life, they must acquire some level of control over their emotions. The following tips are critical in eliminating emotional and mental distress and helping an empath lead a fulfilling life.

· **Exercise**

Sometimes it's amazing how simple the remedy to a problems can be. If you are stressed at the moment, you don't have to take your credit card and buy some expensive drugs whose side effects are questionable. You only have to put your training shoes on and head to the gym to perform intense workouts. The stress you were battling earlier will go away. Apart from relieving stress, exercising will also boost your brain health, skin health, and immunity.

- **Start a journal**

Writing down our emotional and mental states tends to relieve us of stress. People who keep a diary and write down every incident of their lives are much more likely to have stable thoughts than those who don't keep a diary. Also, a diary will help you understand who you truly are. You will get to study your behavior over time and recognize your tendencies.

- **Create a routine**

Buffalos and elephants wake up and spend their day however they wish. But we are human beings. We need to have a routine or we'll pay a big price. When you have a routine, it means you are aware of how you should spend each moment. If you don't have one, you are likely to become overwhelmed by choices and make the poorest choice. It doesn't cost anything to think through what your average day is like, or rather what it should be like, and then coming up with a routine that will guide you through the day.

- **Spend time with your family and friends**

Sometimes we underestimate how good relationships are necessary for our emotional health. We tend to be genuinely happy when surrounded by our blood relations. We also tend to be happy when surrounded by our friends. So, if one is going through a stressful moment, the answer is to simply seek contact with family or friends to regain an emotional balance.

- **Be an early riser**

If you are sleeping like an old lion, you are obviously going to have issues. When you are an early riser, you get to condition your mind for the day ahead and work toward achieving important goals. Rising early will give you a head start, and you are likely to run into more opportunities as opposed to waking up later in the day. Early risers perform the heavy tasks and spread the easy tasks through the rest of the day, thus eliminating emotional distress.

- **Create a challenge for yourself every day**

Perhaps the reason you commonly feel distressed is that you don't feel like a winner or achiever. One way to overcome this feeling of inadequacy is by creating a daily challenge for yourself. You can challenge yourself to earn something, make a certain amount of money, approach people and find out about their day, and so on. Basically, it's about improving your emotional health.

- **Face your reality**

It doesn't matter what's going on in your life right now. It doesn't matter what you have lost or what kind of challenges you are facing. But it will do you a world of good if you summon the courage to face your reality and look for solutions to your problems. Some people who are not courageous enough will turn to addiction and vices to escape reality. But the result is that they will actually worsen their situation. If you can muster the courage to face your problems, you have won half the battle.

·   **Listen to refreshing music**

Music is food for the soul. Ensure that you listen to music every now and again to keep your spirits up. Also, when you are battling a major stressful condition or when you have lost your confidence, listen to upbeat music to improve your mood.

·   **Take good care of yourself**

When you are going through emotional distress, it can be tempting to lock yourself away and never step outside again. Get rid of those thoughts and start taking great care of yourself. Take the time to prepare the meals you fancy, buy the clothes that bring out your charisma, and groom yourself to the heavens. Don't make the mistake of ignoring your needs. When you take great care of yourself, it will help you develop a positive image and discourage stress from invading your mind.

· **Relax**

If you are experiencing emotional distress, you will need to relax so you can feel better about yourself. One of the common reasons why people feel distressed is due to overworking themselves. But when you take that well-deserved rest, you will recover your energy and go back to being productive.

· **Meditation**

The importance of this exercise when it comes to getting rid of emotional and mental distress cannot be overstated. Meditation is a mental exercise that helps in cleansing our minds and bodies. This practice has maintained its relevance since ancient times. There are ways you can practice meditation, and each of them is designed for a particular purpose.

A simple meditation exercise involves finding a comfortable place, assuming a relaxing pose, closing your eyes, and then focusing on your breath. Every breath you inhale and exhale should take away your worries, anxieties, and pain, and eventually leave you feeling rejuvenated.

The beauty of meditation is that you can perform it almost anywhere, even at your place of work. So, if you feel exhausted, burdened, or depressed, you only have to meditate and you'll be well again.

· **Get rid of distractions**

Sometimes, you may acquire stress as a result of the distractions around you. These distractions may be in the form of TV, radio, and phone. If you are looking to meditate and relax, these distractions will hinder you from doing it. So, ensure you have removed them.

· **Increase in concentration**

Learn to increase your focus and concentrate on your tasks because that's what will give you results. If you fail to concentrate, you are likely to fall short of your goals. One of the biggest causes of distress are unmet goals. But if you are a winner, you are likely to develop a positive mindset, and life will be pleasant. One of the best ways to develop focus is by being a starter. When you show up at your place of work, just throw yourself into work as opposed to succumbing to distractions.

- **Stop procrastinating**

Procrastination is closely related to a lack of focus. If you are a procrastinator, you're surely doing yourself a disservice. Procrastination holds you back from fulfilling your important life goals. A procrastinator tends to hold things off that they should do today for tomorrow, and then tomorrow they repeat the same trend, and the day after tomorrow...when they finally run out of time, now that's when they start rushing over things, while others simply give up because the task ahead is enormous, and they haven't got the time. Procrastination always ends badly.

Notes

_____

_____

_____

_____

_____

_____

Chapter 13:
The Psychology of Empathy

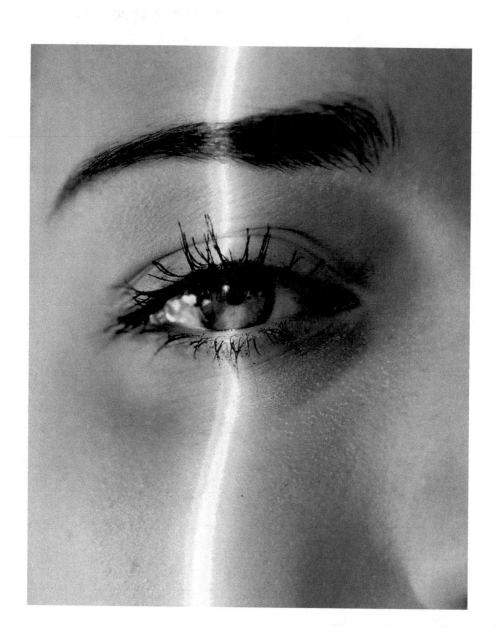

Empath vs. Sympathy

E mpathy is the ability to feel another person's emotions, thus making the empath more understanding. Empathy is very useful in situations when you're upset. People will tell you they understand how you feel and empathize with you. However, this isn't sympathy. Sympathy means actually feeling the same emotions as someone else without having to experience it yourself. Thus, sympathy is a different reaction than empathy.

Empathy is often confused with sympathy. For example, when someone doesn't seem to empathize with you, you might feel they really don't care about you or your problems. However, their lack of empathy could just mean that they can't really relate to what you're saying; so it doesn't feel as personal to them as it does to you. This isn't necessarily a bad thing.

Empathy and Nonverbal Communication

Emotions are contagious, so when we see someone else in pain, we feel bad for them. We can also feel the hope they feel. We want to reach out to comfort them and make everything better because it's just not fair if you see someone suffer, and there's nothing you can do about it.

Empathy is different from sympathy in many ways. When the emotions are similar, both sympathy and empathy are the same. But when the emotions are different, such as in the example above, empathy is different from sympathy.

Because of this, people react differently. They might want to be sympathetic and help you out as much as possible. However, if they can't really understand what you're feeling and they see that their help isn't really needed, they may not feel it necessary to keep trying.

Emotions can also be contagious through facial expressions. If you see someone smile or laugh, you might feel like smiling or laughing too. However, if you see someone crying or get upset in some way, that can be contagious as well. Lots of people feel bad for the person and want to comfort him or her.

That's why there aren't enough words to describe our emotions perfectly, and it isn't possible for us to fully show how we feel through words alone. The most important thing is that we understand that our feelings are communicated, and we can comfort each other.

Emotions are often uncontrollable. It's impossible to control what you feel in any given situation. There will always be misunderstandings, and people won't always react the way you want. However, it's still very important to understand how people react to different emotions so you're able to make a connection and communicate.

Facial expressions are nonverbal communication, and they play a big role in how other people react to you. The main thing you need to learn is that facial expressions aren't the same for everyone. There are some that only certain cultures understand or can be misinterpreted depending on the situation.

While it might be tempting to smile or laugh when someone else does, not everyone is comfortable with that. Sometimes, people are in a bad mood and don't want someone to make them smile when they don't feel like it. And sometimes, you might see someone smiling or laughing when they're not happy at all.

How other people can help for us to feel better

The best thing that we can do for each other is to understand how we can help one another out better. When we look at a situation from another person's point of view, we can see how they might be feeling and empathize with them.

To achieve this, it's important to break down the process of communication so we can fully understand what the other person is trying to say. Most of the time, people don't really know how they feel or what they want to say. They just try to communicate as best they can. Instead of assuming that they know what they're trying to say, we can ask questions to understand them better and empathize with them.

It's also very important to point out when there's a misunderstanding. The best way of doing this is to break it down into details so you can clearly communicate what you mean. It's always frustrating when someone doesn't really get where you're coming from, and they keep telling you the same thing over and over again. When you're frustrated, it can be helpful to take a deep breath and explain the situation in as much detail as possible.

Other people can help you with your emotions by understanding you better. Sometimes, you might not know how to tell someone what you want. And sometimes, other people don't know what they should do to help someone else with their problems.

Notes

Conclusion

Thank you for making it through the end. When you are an empath, you find it difficult to make and maintain relationships. This does not mean you are weak, not at all. Empaths have very a high emotional intelligence that allows them to relate well to others. Being an empath is a blessing that many do not understand.

You radiate peace, compassion, and empathy to others in every dimension. You are a highly sensitive individual with a tendency to feel the emotions of those around you. You are more affected by negative than positive energy but are able to bring out the best in others. This is a skill you possess and should learn to harness.

This sensitivity gives you the ability to identify with others and feel their emotions. Likewise, your ability enables you to sense dangers and know what is best for everyone around you. Being an empath means that you are a natural healer. You have the touch and power to heal emotionally or physically. You can use it to make people happy. This is a skill you should learn to use wisely and not abuse just because you can.

Empaths have a very high sense of discernment that allows them to determine what is real and what is not. This means that you can easily distinguish a lie from a truthful statement. You also sense when someone is in distress and feel the emotional pain of others.

When you are an empath, you should protect your energy and from negative people who want to drain you emotionally. You should also avoid toxic relationships where people use your empathy against you.

The goal of this book is to help you understand your friends and family better by knowing how they feel. Share this guide with them, and if they accept it, happy reading. If they don't, then know that you are at least sharing an understanding of yourself as well.

Thank you for making it this far. I hope this book has been helpful in some way. Take care and know that there are many people who love you no matter what, and it is always their pleasure to hear from your side of the world.

How to Set Boundaries

A Beginners Guide to Set Healthy Boundaries with
Toxic People and Enforcing Your Standards

Introduction

It's a Friday afternoon. You're working late, trying to catch up on your job because you agreed to help a coworker with a project. You're exhausted and you want to go home, but you can't because you are supposed to stop by a family member's house to let their dog out and water the plants. You have to cook dinner for your family this evening and wake up early tomorrow morning because your spouse wants help with a renovation this weekend. Your project is due Monday, and your kid is having a bake sale, which you signed up for because the teacher asked a few weeks ago.

Does this sound familiar? You're exhausted, and you have a full schedule of plans ahead. You don't know when you're going to get some peace again, and there's no end in sight. Then someone comes up to you and asks for a favor. For some crazy reason, you say yes. You may seem to have a problem saying no. You see, people in the world will mold themselves to be whoever they need to be in front of others. These people, called people-pleasers, can:

- Find it difficult to say no because of feeling too worried or guilty about others' feelings and opinions.
- Say yes too quickly and find it hard to achieve everything they signed up for.
- Use small lies and excuses to get out of situations that they have overbooked.
- Commonly say sorry.

- Have a tough time accepting help and compliments.
- Rescue people often.
- Say yes because they're searching for validation and purpose.
- Commonly be exhausted and burnt out.
- Have trouble communicating what they need or want to be happy.
- Feel like their emotions and opinions don't matter.

Some people will travel to the end of the world to make others happy. Some will swim oceans and walk miles to please those around them. While this may seem like a great quality to have, it can take a toll. When you're always the giver, you might be a people pleaser. We run around trying to make everyone happy. We think we're okay, and we will get a break once we are finished, but when you're a people pleaser, you never get a break.

Having all or some of the characteristics above can predict that you're a people pleaser. Being a people pleaser or a giver means you almost constantly have something going on. Whether you are swamped with volunteer committees at your kids' school or buried with projects at work, you are a busy person. You want to learn more about what it means to be a people pleaser.

1. You want to learn more about yourself.

2. You want to make changes to your life for the better.

People pleasers are also called givers because they give away parts of themselves to fit into communities and conversations. Givers will give their health, wealth, time, and resources to make others happy and comfortable.

You are a people pleaser if others are consistently taking advantage of you. Here's a big one: you don't ask for help. No matter how overwhelmed you get, asking for help is your last option. Then when you do ask for help, you feel awful for asking. It's a lose-lose situation.

But let's not forget that most of us do want to help people. It can be our passion to help others with what they need. People pleasers can be a great help for others. The problems arise when we are sacrificing too much of ourselves. These problems get worse when we lose ourselves trying to please others.

People pleasers are "givers," and those that are being helped are "takers." While givers are set in stone about giving (and takers are set in stone for taking), we need a little more balance. If people are constantly giving, there will be no one to take. Givers must get accustomed to taking occasionally. Even a flower must "take" from its environment to "give" pollen to bees.

As a people pleaser, it's important to take care of yourself. Being a "superhuman" may feel good, but accepting everything asked of you can take a toll on your health—emotionally, physically, mentally, and spiritually.

Chapter 1:
What are Boundaries?

B oundaries are often mentioned in self-help books and relationship counseling sessions. What are boundaries? How do they relate to mental health? How do they benefit relationships? This book will explore all these questions and offer insight into how we can better understand them in our own lives.

Boundaries help us to recognize and set limits with those around us. They allow us to maintain our mental, emotional, physical, and spiritual health. It is important for people in relationships to have boundaries and apply them in their lives. If you're unsure what boundaries are or how they can benefit your relationships, this chapter will give you some great examples!

Boundaries are an unavoidable part of relationships. They help us to maintain a good balance between the people in our lives and ourselves. There are different types of boundaries, and they all serve a purpose. Boundaries aren't a bad thing, and they prepare us for the world; we need to learn how to use them in ways that will help us grow as individuals and as a relationship.

Here is an example of how much we can take from relationships when we don't have boundaries. A friend was almost killed because she let her emotions get out of control and ignored her boyfriend's boundaries. She went into this relationship with boundaries in place, but she eventually let those boundaries go away to please her boyfriend instead of herself. This is an example of letting someone else's boundaries take priority over your own.

People often give each other their time and emotional energy without thinking about the consequences. The person who limits their emotional involvement with someone is the one that will end up with less hurt and more benefits.

How important is it for people in relationships to have boundaries? It's very important! Our lives inevitably involve relationships, so we must learn how to have healthy boundaries early on. Suppose we don't learn how to set healthy limits. In that case, we can unknowingly end up pushing others away or looking for more harmful behaviors in our relationships because of our inability to cope.

It's not just emotions that set boundaries but also physical, mental, emotional, and spiritual concerns. A wonderful way to maintain a healthy balance in relationships is to know which boundaries are important and which ones you can let go of.

Boundaries are important for relationships because they allow us to feel good about ourselves without being hurtful to others or ourselves. They help us avoid confusion and fight for our own needs instead of trying to please others all the time. Relationships without boundaries can lead to conflict, confusion, resentment, and jealousy. To avoid this, you need to learn what boundaries are and how you can apply them in your life.

TYPES OF BOUNDARIES

Physical Boundaries:

These are the most common boundaries set in relationships. Physical boundaries preserve our physical space and protect us from physical harm. They define where we can and can't go, touch, or play with. We set physical boundaries to protect ourselves from unwanted contact, pain, disease, and even death. Sometimes an injury or illness is a good thing because it can force us to find a healthy balance between social interactions and our own needs. We find out what kind of person we are when we have to make decisions for our bodies, and they eventually teach us who we are as a person.

For instance, a fence is a boundary between two properties. The physicality of the boundary can act as a signal to ward off unwanted people and animals. It also delimits who is inside and outside an area.

While clearer in their definition, physical boundaries create severe isolation from the people outside of them when there is no access point or gateway for pouring in new perspectives and ideas. Additionally, physical boundaries may be more difficult to change depending on their location, which might be necessary for security reasons or aesthetic nuances.

Emotional Boundaries:

Emotional boundaries prevent emotional distress. Emotional boundaries are important because they help us avoid manipulation and abuse in a relationship. We don't want people to treat us the way they do because it doesn't feel good anymore. Emotional boundaries can be hard to set up as we want people to love and accept us for who we are, but everyone is different. Emotional boundaries allow us to have healthy self-esteem. If someone constantly ignores our feelings or treats us like they're above us, it's probably best to take a step back from that relationship and try our hardest not to get involved.

Mental Boundaries:

Like emotional boundaries, mental boundaries also help us avoid being controlled by another person. You set mental boundaries when you don't want to be messed with mentally, as in "Don't try to play mind games with me." Mental messages are probably the most important ones we get from others because they either make or break our day. If you're mentally hurt and beat up from your environment, and there's no one there to protect you, you're going to fall apart emotionally. To avoid this, we need mental boundaries so the negative thoughts will have a harder time making us feel bad.

In relationships, this can be the agreement between two people not to betray each other emotionally by revealing certain thoughts or feelings.

Spiritual Boundaries:

Boundaries aren't just for people; and they can also be for ourselves. You set spiritual boundaries when you don't want to bend over backward for God anymore. Instead of giving into fears or worries, you're going to have a new outlook on your situation and your life in general. You're going to learn how precious your time is and make sure to use it wisely. Everything we do in life needs boundaries, even our spiritual lives!

People in a relationship need to have boundaries regarding religion and spirituality because it helps them find out what they believe. If there is no mention of God or religion, it can lead to confusion, opinion, judgment, and even judgemental behavior.

It's important to know that you can mix and match boundaries and apply them in your relationships. It's just like a relationship with someone else; the more you work together, the better it will be.

Boundaries also refer to everything from your thoughts, beliefs, values, opinions, and how you want to live your life. If you're with somebody who likes to criticize you all the time, you should leave them because they aren't respecting your boundaries and are hurting you as a person. They might think that their opinion is the only one that matters. They may want things done their way all the time, which can lead to confusion and problems, especially if people don't like being told what to do when it comes to relationship problems in general.

How do you know if you have boundaries?

If you're in a relationship with someone who doesn't have any boundaries, there's no telling what they'll do or how they'll treat you. It can be easy to assume that they don't have boundaries because you don't know what they're like and they haven't acted out in any way yet; however, there are some ways you can tell if someone has boundaries.

When someone is in a relationship and doesn't talk about how they feel, they're likely not open up. They may be afraid to speak up for themselves with people who remind them of past experiences or thoughts. They may also be afraid that the person they're with will make fun of them. People need to speak up and let others know about how they feel to help them feel closer to their partners.

Suppose someone is in a relationship with someone who doesn't have boundaries and walks on eggshells around them. In that case, it's likely because they're afraid of upsetting them if they don't respect boundaries, they are most likely not respectful of themselves. If you're in a relationship and have boundaries, but your partner doesn't, it's likely because they've been hurt in the past and are afraid to be open with people now. They may assume that if they don't have boundaries, they won't be found out. People need to understand that no one will hurt them if they do have boundaries in place.

If someone is in a relationship with someone who doesn't have boundaries and walks all over them, it's likely because they don't have any. They may also be afraid of upsetting their partner because they know their partner won't address or confront the situation. They may think that it's easier to let the other person do as they please rather than stand up for themselves.

They also assume that if they do something wrong, the partner in the relationship will call them out on their actions. People need to understand that nothing can replace speaking up for yourself and what you believe in, even if someone else doesn't agree with you.

It's also important for such people to know that they are not alone in their opinions or feelings and to believe that everyone is on the same page. It's okay to believe that something should be done a certain way and not ask why. It'll make the person feel better knowing they're not the only one who feels this way if they put a lot of pressure on themselves because everyone else thinks differently. That's called bullying, making these people feel ashamed of their opinions because having boundaries means not being bullied or belittled.

When we can respect someone else's boundaries, we show that we care about them and their feelings, even if we don't agree with them. It will also bring down the negativity in a relationship which will lead to better communication and understanding.

Chapter 2:
Guidelines for Relationship Boundaries

T o set the right type of personal boundaries, you need to follow a few rules, remembering that these are merely guidelines and not stringent dictates. You can use them as a reference and formulate your boundaries through understanding what boundaries stand for. These are some general rules and regulations for you to adhere to set your boundaries. You will have to tweak them to suit the relationship in your life.

BOUNDARY SETTING RULES

Identifying the needs

Before setting boundaries, identify the various relationships in your life and the type of relationship. Identify the needs of every relationship and decide where lines need to be drawn. This is especially important if it's a new relationship and you are not sure of where you stand yet.

You have to be smart about it and know where to draw your personal and emotional lines. Perhaps writing down a list of names would help establish the dynamics between each group of people. Split these into family, friends, close friends, new friends, teachers, colleagues, etc. No one but you know what these groups are because others are not standing in your shoes. Thus, decide upon the groups that best suit your life.

Self- awareness

You have to know where you stand to set the right boundaries. Ask yourself how much you need to be in control and if you are in a good position to lay down the rules. Self-awareness allows you to evaluate every relationship you have. Do you cringe when someone telephones? Why? People need to respect your need for boundaries. Those people you avoid are trying to break down your resistance and get through the fences you have built to protect your privacy. Self-awareness can objectively and accurately identify one's own emotions, strengths, limitations, skills, and personality traits. Self-aware people have a deep understanding of themselves that enables them to make good decisions about their lives.

Self-awareness is essential in personal and professional relationships, and it is a critical factor for personal growth. It allows people to control their impulses, deal with change, overcome denial, and consider the consequences of their actions. "Self-awareness" is not synonymous with "self-consciousness." Self-conscious people are preoccupied with how they appear to others, whereas self-aware people are more concerned with understanding how they feel. They know what motivates them and are aware of their values. People who lack self-awareness have distorted views of themselves that create problems in many areas of their lives.

Self-awareness is important because it helps you understand how others see in action and let you appreciate your strengths and weaknesses, make well-calculated decisions, and improve your relationships with other people. If this is important to you, we recommend working on your self-awareness! Find time for things like meditation or going for a run every day...

Put yourself first

Regardless of what type of relationship you are examining, you have to learn to put yourself first. It does not matter that you love your spouse or partner very much. What matters is that you love yourself first. Self-love determines your strength.

Only then can you do justice to your relationship with other people. People often have trouble with this concept, though self-love doesn't mean vanity. It means self-respect and self-esteem. You have to think yourself worthy, or how else would you expect your partner to love you? He/she loves you because you are worthy. You only become worthy by respecting yourself and learning your value. Anything less than that is giving less than you should be. That would mean your partner is only getting a part of your potential. Self-love means seeing the good side of yourself and letting others see it too.

Working together

When setting boundaries, it is imperative to discuss it with and involve the other person in question. You cannot make decisions for both of you by yourself, especially if it's a mutual idea. Sit down and work together to establish the limits. Often families have family meetings to discuss things like this.

Between the two of you, create a compromise that work regarding boundaries. Imagine dating someone with absolutely no boundaries at all. You would never know when they could turn up. You would never know when you had time to wash your hair or even clean your teeth. Boundaries are essential to every relationship.

Working together helps considerably. A wife who feels put upon because she is left with all the housework and care of the children should discuss acceptable boundaries to give her adequate freedom. Without this freedom, she may fall into a state of stagnation and feel resentment at not doing things that she considers necessary for her welfare.

Start on a small scale

It is no secret that it is better to start on a small scale. Conduct a trial run and see how it goes. Whether it is for a spouse or your children, try setting small boundaries first and then move towards the larger ones. Try setting a few physical boundaries first and then start setting emotional ones. For example, if you have a particularly negative friend, make sure you get some days when he/she leaves you alone. If you need space away from the kids, find them an activity that gives you space and make sure that they respect it. Every day of your life, you set boundaries. If you don't set these up, relationships with others falter.

Be reasonable

Regardless where boundaries are being imposed, remember that boundaries are a two-way street. Be mature in your approach and prepared to handle any situation that may arise within a relationship after the boundaries have been made clear.

It may be worthwhile experimenting with kids and helping them understand boundaries. When they want a little bit of "me" time, respect it. The kid who is embarrassed because his mom insists on kissing him outside school should be given the respect he is asking for.

He is growing up, and that embarrassment is something he shouldn't have to face. Given a choice, he will probably be the first to kiss his mom after school or when the time is right. He sets up the barrier for arrival at school, a reasonable one for a growing child.

Be assertive

Once you decide to draw certain boundaries, be assertive and tell your partner that he/she needs to express their own boundaries assertively. Sometimes, it is important to be assertive so that no misunderstandings come from those imposed boundaries. If you want your partner to build a certain wall or draw a particular emotional line, make a demand for it and give him/her a feasible and acceptable reason for your demand.

For example, your spouse may want you to go out visiting when you do not want to. Explain that you don't want to and explain why. Your partner then gains a better understanding than if you simply refused to adhere to his wishes, which builds resentment. Being assertive takes practice, but if you can logically explain why something is unacceptable to you and allow your partner to do the same, you open up communication channels that will make the relationship more honest.

Move on

Move on and leave the past in the past. We often hear this sentiment from friends, therapists, and, most importantly, those who know us best. The idea behind this statement is that by moving on and not dwelling on the past, we can heal quicker and find happiness again.

In a sense, I agree with this statement. My own life has been one of disappointment and betrayal. Moving on to a better way of living is the only way to happiness as I learned. However, to completely write my past off is impossible for me. If I throw away the past that shaped me into who I am today, then who will ever know why things are the way they are now?

If we all could write our past off so easily, then there would be no such thing as true forgiveness. Without holding onto my past and remembering what happened to me, I would not forgive those that were truly at fault for my pain and suffering.

Learn to move on from past experiences and don't hold on to memories and events that had a deep bearing on you. Also, when establishing emotional boundaries, do not judge your partner for his/her past. People often use things like this as leverage to get what they want. That is not fair, and if you need to do that, you are no doubt in the wrong kind of relationship. Imagine if your spouse did that to you. It's unacceptable.

Moving on involves forgiving and forgetting. If you cannot do this, then the relationship will suffer as a direct result.

Moral values

Think carefully of the moral values you were taught as a child and consider when you first set boundaries. These were set for a good reason, and usually, the rights and wrongs you were taught as a child set you up with standards for life. These help you establish boundaries that work and are acceptable to others with the same set of values.

They have moral expectations of you. Moral obligations and values are usually very easy to maintain. If yours turns out to be different from theirs, respect them and do not mock whatthey see as right and wrong. Instead, understand that the differences in your moral values are simply statements of who you are and who they are. They should never create barriers between you.

Spirituality

Some boundaries are drawn for religious reasons. If you are a staunch believer in God, you must abide by the holy texts' rules. Most talk about abstaining from adultery and also not bringing emotional harm to others. Boundaries between different religions can set up a lot of unnecessary misunderstandings. Instead of preaching to others and imposing upon their space, it's necessary to respect that their beliefs might be every bit as important to them as yours are to you. Thus, although the boundaries you are setting are not religiously based, they should respect others' beliefs.

Sharing your religious beliefs with your children would be perfectly acceptable, although quoting religious text at a friend who has erred would certainly get in the way of the friendship. All she/he wants is understanding and perhaps forgiveness. Righteous indignation and throwing religious text at a friend won't help him/her to feel better about the error that has been made. Helping friends understand an alternative with compassion in your heart is a far better way to go forward, allowing spirituality and humility to guide you.

Seek help

If you're in a situation where neither you nor your partner can agree on something, it's probably because you are both too close to the situation. In such a case, asking for expert help makes good sense. That outsider can be any mature person in your life who will genuinely help you with common-sense solutions you will both listen to. You can also seek professional help to help you express yourself better if you cannot come to a mutual understanding. This doesn't just apply to a love relationship. This can apply to a parent-child relationship, a teacher-student relationship, or any relationship causing problems.

Learn to say "No."

If you feel that someone is hurting you, physically and mentally, and is crossing all boundaries, say "no." Don't wait for it to pass or find a way around it. Remember, you have set the boundaries for yourself, and if they are violated, you need to establish a definite answer.

People can be considered as "doormats" and put upon because they don't set boundaries. If you find yourself being asked to do things you don't want to do, learning to say "no" helps to set a boundary that

138

others will understand and appreciate. It doesn't mean that you will lose worthy friendships. You will gain more respect when people know that you are sensible enough to draw the line.

Be cautious

People who drop boundaries often find that they make themselves more vulnerable, and this vulnerability leaves them open to hurt. Throwing caution to the wind is acceptable sometimes, as long as you know the potential outcome.

Time

Setting rigid and clear boundaries takes time. Don't expect to establish them overnight. How much time it takes completely depends on your boundary-setting ability, and the time you take to let down your defenses. Take your time.

Chapter 3:
Why People have Unreasonable Boundaries?

I f you have ever come across a person with narrow boundaries, think about why they are that way. Many things cause narrow boundaries. For example, someone might have been raised with a lack of boundaries and knows no other way to live in the world. Or some people might not know that some things just aren't okay to do. Whatever it is, it might need to be addressed before you can call the person's boundary unreasonable.

Why do People Have Unreasonable or no Boundaries?

Growing up in a family where the parents had difficulty setting their boundaries is likely to pass it on. Children might have been raised to treat all people the same way. Another reason is the fear of being controlled. Some people are afraid of being controlled by others, so they never want to control anyone else by setting boundaries.

Examples of Unreasonable Boundaries

An example of someone with narrow boundaries is when they have their cell phone on at all times. They don't want it out of their sight for any reason. They take it everywhere and then resent you for doing the same thing. The problem is that this person doesn't even like being in touch that much. They feel overwhelmed by other people's demands and requests for their time, attention, and energy.

People with narrow boundaries might want to have sex with whomever they want whenever they want and then get mad at a refusal. They don't respect themselves or their bodies, so they feel they have the right to use people as much as they want. Hence, it can be hard for people with narrow boundaries to meet people for the first time in person since they never know how someone will react to demands for sex.

Negative Examples of People with Unreasonable Boundaries

No matter how much you plead, beg, and apologize, you just can't make the other person happy. You will do anything to make them happy, but it doesn't work because they are unreasonable. You remind them of someone else who did something terrible to them in their past who they can't forgive. The relationship ends badly, and you feel like there is nothing left to live for since this person won't love you back because you aren't good enough for them.

Positive Examples of People with Unreasonable Boundaries

You have finally found someone who respects you. You can never do anything wrong in their eyes because they love you for who you are. However, they are a little insecure and afraid of letting anyone else in. They feel this person is the only one who could ever be good to them, but it will all go away if they don't let them in. This makes it difficult for them to keep a relationship going. Still, if they can find their balance and continue being happy with themselves and the other person, your relationship will work out great!

Staying Out of the Way of Unreasonable Boundaries

It can be hard to stay out of the way of an unreasonable person. But it is worth it. If you are a reasonable person, you don't want to make their boundaries more difficult than they need be. Instead, you want to stick to your own set and see if a reasonable solution can be reached. Once you keep out of their way and have left this situation, you may find that it was not be as bad as you had thought, and it will stop bothering you so much as a result.

Get Someone to Stop Having Unreasonable Boundaries

Unreasonable boundaries tend to come from somewhere, so it's always best to try and work from where the problem originated before trying anything else. This isn't always possible, but it's a good place to start. These are a couple of ways get someone to stop having narrow boundaries.

First, help them learn the correct way to have boundaries. This can be hard if they have been taught the wrong way all their lives, but they might be open to learning how some things should be. You could even ask them which type they want to work on in the future and then offer a few insights on adapting better.

This can sometimes help you go through some of your upsetting situations and get through some of theirs. When they are done with this break, you both must pick up the pieces again - not knocking anything over and making things worse than before! It will be a little uncomfortable while it lasts, but once things settle down, you'll both be fine talking again.

If they want to drop you in the middle of a request, take things slow. You will be able to pick up where you left off eventually, but don't push it if they aren't ready for that yet. If they are unreasonably rejecting your end goal because of your boundaries, you should try to find out what their real concerns might be.

Chapter 4:
Boundary Problems

I n the context of rules and ethics, a boundary problem occurs when someone feels like an individual is overstepping their limits. These can be anything from exceeding authority to being too personal. Each individual has their boundaries, and even a violation will vary according each person's hierarchy of what is important.

Boundary problems occur for many reasons, which lead to different types of violations. If a boundary is crossed with someone else's property, this can lead to theft or trespassing, and if it is crossed through a person's boundaries, it could be seen as harassment. Boundary problems can occur for a variety of different reasons.

Examples

In my own experience, boundary problems typically occur when someone is crossing the line by doing something deemed inappropriate. These instances can range from sexual harassment to discussing past relationships or even divulging personal information that they should know better not to disclose. In other cases, it may be an innocent gesture like offering a hug or asking for permission before touching the person's arms. In each of these scenarios, the act itself is harmless, but it is a violation because the other does not want that particular action.

In other situations, more serious boundary problems occur because of repeated actions that are perceived as harassment or abuse. These may include sexual harassment in the workplace, stalking outside of work, and crimes like date rape. We may even feel violated when someone physically comes to our home but doesn't knock or attempt to communicate they are at the door.

Origins

Boundary problems arise in each of us from different experiences with our families, culture, context, and life. If we were raised with healthy boundaries in place, we know the difference between appropriate and inappropriate behavior. The same goes for people who grew up in abusive situations; they can have difficulty understanding what is appropriate.

When I was young, I was taught to respect my elders and be honest and polite. As a result, I tended to be respectful and worked hard not to offend. These are all positive qualities that go along with healthy boundaries. However, sometimes they worked against me when people pushed my limits and crossed lines.

Furthermore, sometimes people wonder if they have crossed a line or not. In these cases, the most important thing is to consider the person you are dealing with and ask directly if they feel comfortable with something you are doing. If they say no, it is probably best not to do that action again and make sure you have their permission going forward.

Limitations

There are no finite rules when it comes to boundaries. Each person is unique has a different set of boundaries personal to them. Being considerate of someone's feelings is as important as accepting boundaries as personal choices. Just because someone believes something is inappropriate or unacceptable does not mean that you should stop doing it. Boundary problems should never be taken personally, and we need to remember that everyone is entitled to their personal beliefs and opinions.

Solutions

In many cases, boundary problems can be difficult to solve. Even if the person feels comfortable talking with you about an issue, they may not realize what they are doing is wrong or crossing lines. In this case, it is important to explain your position and where you stand. In other instances, the person may see that they have made a mistake and apologize for their actions. In these situations, forgiveness is important in letting go of a negative situation. Either way, with patience and communication, we can work through most of the boundary problems in our lives.

In other cases, especially where harassment or abuse occurs, it is important to seek help from authorities like counselors or police officers. Many who have been abused do not realize the severity of the situation, and if they have a history of being victimized, some may feel hesitant to come forward with their complaints, but it may be necessary if they are to be completely free from any kind of inappropriate behavior in the future.

Collaboration

Since boundary problems always occur when someone feels like they are crossing a line or being too personal, we need to encourage understanding and communication instead of aggression or disrespect. These issues only become even more difficult on an interpersonal level because we all want to be respected as individuals and love each other. We must remember that we are not "them" or "different" from them and they are just human beings like us.

If we can work together to understand one another instead of struggling with our bad behavior, we will build a better world. As the saying goes, we must "love thy neighbor as thyself." Rather than fight and quarrel over boundaries, why don't we become more considerate of each other's feelings and work together to create a society where everyone can be respected, understood, and have a good life.

Chapter 5:
Borderline Personality Disorder

A borderline personality disorder is the most common among the different types of personality disorders listed in the revised Diagnostic and Statistical Manual of Mental Disorders (DSM-iv-tr). Physicians and use this manual as do registered psychologists when they make a mental health diagnosis.

The DSM-iv-tr defines a personality disorder as "an enduring pattern of inner experience and behavior that deviates markedly from the expectations of the individual's culture are pervasive and inflexible, has an onset in adolescence or early adulthood, is stable over time and leads to clinically significant distress or impairment." Someone with a personality disorder generally has difficulty in dealing with relationships and social situations, handling emotions and thoughts, understanding how or why his or her behavior is causing problems, and finds it hard to change to suit different conditions.

The Origins Of BPD

Borderline Personality Disorder, like all other primary psychiatric disorders, is caused by a a complex combination of genetic, social, and psychological factors. All modern theories now agree that multiple causes must interact with one another for the disorder to become manifest. There are, however, known risk factors for the development of BPD, including those present at birth, called temperaments, experiences occurring in childhood, and sustained environmental influences.

Inborn Biogenetic Temperaments

The degree to which Borderline Personality Disorder is caused by genetic factors, called the "level of heritability," is estimated to be 52-68%. This is about the same as bipolar disorder. What is believed to be inherited are the biogenetic dispositions, i.e., temperaments (or, as noted above, phenotypes), for Affective Dysregulation, Impulsivity, and Interpersonal Hypersensitivity. For children with these inborn dispositions, environmental factors can then significantly delimit or exacerbate them into adult BPD. But also, a more BPD-specific type is inherited that glues these phenotypes together.

Many studies have shown that disorders of emotional regulation, interpersonal hypersensitivity or impulsivity are disproportionately higher in relatives of BPD patients. The affect/emotion temperament predisposes individuals to be easily upset, angry, depressed, and anxious. The impulsivity temperament predisposes individuals to act without thinking of the consequences or even to seek dangerous activities purposefully. The interpersonal hypersensitivity temperament probably starts with extreme sensitivity to separations or rejections.

Another theory has proposed that patients with BPD are born with excessive aggression, which is genetically based (as opposed to being environmental in origin). A child born with a cheerful, warm, calm, or passive temperament would be unlikely to develop BPD.

149

The standard neurological function is needed for such complex tasks as impulse control, regulation of emotions, and perception of social cues. Studies of BPD patients have identified an increased incidence of neurological dysfunctions, often subtle, that are discernible on close examination. The most considerable portion of the brain is the cerebrum, where information is interpreted from the senses, and conscious thoughts and planned behavior emanate. Preliminary studies have found that individuals with BPD have a diminished response to emotionally intense stimulation in the cerebrum's planning/organizing areas.

The lower levels of brain activity may promote impulsive behavior. The limbic system, located at the center of the brain, is sometimes thought of as "the emotional brain" and consists of the amygdala, hippocampus, thalamus, hypothalamus, and parts the brain stem. There is evidence that in response to emotional arousal, the amygdala is particularly active in BPD persons.

Psychological Factors

Like most other mental illnesses, Borderline Personality Disorder does not appear to originate during a specific, discrete development phase. Recent studies have suggested that pre-borderline children fail to learn accurate ways to identify feelings or to accurately attribute motives in themselves and others (often called failures of "mentalization"). Such children fail to develop essential mental capacities that constitute a stable sense of self and make themselves or others invalidating environment. This occurs when a child is led to

150

believe that their feelings, thoughts, and perceptions are not real or do not matter.

About 70% of people with BPD report a history of physical and sexual abuse. Childhood traumas may contribute to symptoms such as alienation, the desperate search for protective relationships, and the eruption of intense feelings that characterize BPD. Still, since relatively few physically or sexually abused people develop the borderline disorder (or any other psychiatric disorder), it is essential to consider temperamental disposition. Since BPD can develop without such experiences, these traumas are not sufficient or enough by themselves to explain the illness. Still, sexual or other abuse can be the "ultimate" invalidating environment.

Indeed, when the abuser is a caretaker, the child may need to engage in splitting (denying feelings of hatred and hate to preserve the idea of being loved). Approximately 30% of people with BPD have experienced early parental loss or prolonged separation from their parents; experiences believed to contribute to the borderline patient's fears of abandonment.

People with BPD frequently report feeling neglected during their childhood. Sometimes the sources for this sense of neglect are not obvious and might be due to a sense of not being sufficiently understood. Patients often report feeling alienated or disconnected from their families. Often they attribute the difficulties in communication with their parents.

However, the BPD individual's impaired ability to describe and communicate feelings or needs or resistance to self-disclosure may be a significant cause of neglect and alienation.

Social and Cultural Factors

Evidence shows that a borderline personality is found in about 2-4% of the population. There may be societal and cultural factors that contribute to variations in its prevalence. A fast-paced society, highly mobile, and family situations may be unstable due to divorce, economic factors, or other pressures on the caregivers may encourage this disorder's development.

No matter what age we are, the need for boundaries is an issue for borderline personalities and the unafflicted. We may think someone should know how to behave correctly or how they should act, but often we don't voice that opinion because of fear of confrontation or possible retaliation. People who cross your boundaries or invade your boundaries have some underlying hurt that causes this behavior. It could be wounded self-esteem, a lack of identity, and a huge sense of entitlement and superiority.

We all need boundaries. They help us know where we end and begin; our responsibility towards you ends and yours begins. Boundaries help us define what's acceptable in our relationship with you so that we can move beyond the old boundary issues that inevitably come up before going back to a shared peace.

Boundaries in the family are important, and a lot of times, people have trouble setting them with each other because they are so close. There can be hurt feelings and arguments on all sides when boundaries aren't set with teenagers by parents, spouses by one another, etc. When we don't set boundaries with people close to us, it can lead some to feel that they can take advantage of us or invade our personal space.

Our environment, culture, and society influence how we feel about ourselves, each other, and how we treat one another. Our families usually raise us in this society, shaping the way we look at boundaries in the future.

The Cause of Borderline Personality Disorder

Borderline Personality Disorder usually manifests itself in early adulthood, but its symptoms (e.g., self-harm) can be found in early adolescence. As individuals with BPD age, their symptoms, and the severity of the illness usually diminish. Indeed, about 40-50% of borderline patients remit within two years, and this rate rises to 85% by 10 years. Unlike most other primary psychiatric disorders, those who do remit from BPD don't usually relapse! Studies of BPD have indicated that the first five years of treatment are usually the most crisis-ridden.

A series of intense, unstable relationships that end angrily with subsequent self-destructive or suicidal behaviors are characteristic.

Although such crises may persist for years, a decrease in the frequency and seriousness of self-destructive behaviors and suicidal ideation and acts and a decline in the number of hospitalizations and days in the hospital are early indications of improvement. Whereas about 60% of hospitalized BPD patients are readmitted in the first six months, this rate declines to about 35% in the eighteen months to the two years following an initial hospitalization.

In general, psychiatric care utilization gradually diminishes and increasingly involves briefer, less intensive interventions. Improvements in social functioning proceed more slowly and less thoroughly than do the symptom remissions. Only about 25% of the patients diagnosed with BPD eventually achieve relative stability through close relationships or successful work. Many more have lives that include only limited vocational success and become more avoidant of intimate relationships. While stabilization is expected, and life satisfaction is usually improved, the persisting impairment of the patients' social role functioning is often disappointing.

Suicidality and Self-Harm Behavior

The most dangerous and fear-inducing features of Borderline Personality Disorder are self-harm behavior and the potential for suicide. While 8-10% of the individuals with Borderline Personality Disorder commit suicide, suicidal ideation (thinking and fantasizing about suicide) is pervasive in the borderline population. Deliberate self-harm behaviors (sometimes referred to as parasuicidal acts) are a common feature of BPD, occurring in approximately 75% of patients having the diagnosis and in an even higher percentage for those who have been hospitalized. These behaviors can result in physical scarring and even disabling physical handicaps.

Self-harm behavior takes many forms. Patients with BPD often will self-injure without suicidal intent. The self-injury involves cutting but can include burning, hitting, headbanging, and hair-pulling. Some self-destructive acts are unintentional or not perceived by the patient as self-destructive, such as unprotected sex, driving under the influence, or binging and purging.

Tattoos or pornography with retrospective shame is new variations of this. The motivations for self-injurious behaviors are complex, vary from individual to individual, and may serve different purposes at different times. About 40% of borderline patients' self-harming acts occur during dissociative experiences, times when numbness and emptiness prevail. For these patients, self-injury may be the only way to experience feelings at all. Patients report that causing themselves physical pain generates relief, which temporarily alleviates excruciating psychic pain. Sometimes people with BPD make suicide attempts when they feel alone and unloved or when life feels so excruciatingly painful as to feel unbearable.

There may be a vaguely conceived plan to be rescued, which represents an attempt to relieve the intolerable feelings of being alone byestablishing connections with others. There may even be a neurochemical basis for some self-harming acts; the physical activity may result in a release of certain chemicals (endorphins), which inhibit, at least temporarily, the inner turmoil. Self-destructive behaviors can become addictive, and one of the initial and primary treatment components is to break this cycle.

In addition to substance abuse, major depression can contribute to the risk of suicide. Approximately 50% of people with BPD are experiencing an episode of major depression when they seek treatment, and about 80% have had a major depressive episode in their lifetimes. When depression coexists with the inability to tolerate intense emotion, the urge to act impulsively is exacerbated. It is imperative that treaters evaluate the patient's mood carefully, appreciate the severity of the patient's unhappiness, and recognize that antidepressant medications usually have only modest effects.

Family members are, understandably, tormented by the threat and carrying out such acts. Naturally, reactions vary widely, from wanting to protect the patient to anger at the perceived attention-demanding aspects of the behavior. The risk of suicide incites fear, anger, and helplessness. However, that family members do not need to assume the primary burden to ensure the patient's safety. Whenever there is a perceived threat of harm, or the patient has already engaged in self-harm, a professional should be contacted.

The borderline individual may plead to keep communications or behaviors secret, but safety must be the priority. The patient, treaters, and family cannot work together effectively without honesty, and the threat or occurrence of self-destructive acts cannot be kept secret. This is for the benefit of all concerned. Family members/friends cannot live with these behaviors' specter in their lives, and patients will not progress in their treatment until these behaviors are eliminated.

Once safety concerns have been addressed, through the intervention of professionals, family members/friends can play an essential role in diminishing the likelihood of recurring self destructive threats by merely being present and listening to their loved one, without criticism,rejection or disapproval.

BPD individuals often misuse alcohol or drugs (both prescribed and illegal). This may diminish social anxiety, distance them from painful ruminations, or minimize the intensity of their negative emotions. Often alcohol or drugs have disinhibiting effects that encourage self-injury and suicide attempts, and other self-endangering behaviors.

Chapter 6:
Reasons for Boundary Problems

I f you've been suffering from boundary problems, it's time to get a new plan of attack! Boundary problems can stem from various sources or conditions, and this chapter will give you some ideas for what those boundaries could be. We'll explore how to go about fixing the problem, so your family feels safe and respected as well as avoid doing any harm.

Boundaries are about safety, respect, and well-being. They are about knowing what will or won't work for you and your partner. It is also important to realize that boundaries change over time whether we've been married five years or fifty years. We change, and so does our partner – sometimes daily! So it's always good to revisit what boundaries you need to feel respected, safe, and loved in your relationship.

1. Someone isn't listening or responding well to my needs/feelings/thoughts/concerns.
2. Someone is being too bossy or controlling with me.
3. Someone is not sensitive to my needs.
4. Someone is not respecting me and my independence.
5. Someone is trying to intrude into my life too much.
6. I'm afraid of what will happen if I say, no, or want something different than my partner wants.

7. Someone isn't showing up for me or the relationship in a way that I need or want them to. (includes physical, emotional, spiritual, and sexual issues.)
8. One person seems always to be needing something from the other (parenting, housework, personal time, financial help, etc.).
9. I feel like people are "getting away" with something.
10. Someone is dangerously hurting themselves or others.

Sound familiar? Which one(s) jumps out at you and says, "That's me!"? It's time to take some new action to make things different in your life. Here are a few ideas:

We all have a basic list of needs, and if those needs aren't being met, we have issues with boundaries and often experience boundary problems due to the lack of meeting those needs. The first thing is identifying what your needs are and how they're not being met or respected.

Some simple questions can help you identify your needs and those not being met:

- What do I need to feel safe, respected, and loved?

- How would I like to be treated? (or how do I wish to be treated?)

- What do I need to feel included (or valued) in my relationship?

- How would I like for us to communicate well together?

- What do I need to feel respected emotionally or spiritually in our relationship?

- How would I like to have fun with together or alone as adults without the children? If a parent, what are some ways to take care of yourself? Am I being honest with about not needing to have the children present?

- If married or single, how do I like to be intimate without being embarrassed or feeling pushed to do or say something sexually, physically or emotionally that I don't feel comfortable doing/saying/experiencing?

Resolving Boundary Problem

Once you've identified your needs and those not being met, you've taken a big step in resolving the problem. Now it's time to talk with your partner. It may help figure out what boundaries need to be put in place to ensure that everyone's needs are being met, respected, and responded to appropriately. Here are some ideas for talking (and writing) things through:

- Ask for a "no-blame conversation" or a "no-blame letter writing." This is a direct request that you and your partner try not to blame each other or point fingers while discussing issues of concern. It generally gives everyone permission to be honest without feeling judged or criticized. It's also a way of saying, "It's safe to talk about this." A no-blame conversation may feel awkward at first, but it is possible and will become easier over time.

- It's okay to have an "I" message instead of a "You" message. An "I" message is when you state how you feel instead of complaining or blaming someone else with a judgmental statement. For example, I'm feeling neglected because I haven't seen you in a few days and wanted to spend some time together, but I haven't had the chance today Versus you're always working when I want attention.

- A list of boundaries. Being specific about what you want in a relationship that will allow you to identify and resolve any pain points causing boundary problem. List if you'd like to feel safe, respected, loved.

- "Let's fix this together." This is a way of communicating that you're willing to work on the issue together as a team and going into it with an open mind instead of being defensive and blaming the other.

- "I'm not the only one frustrated." Helping one another realize when we're frustrated or upset can make everyone feel closer. If one partner gets annoyed with another's behavior, they can say, "I'm feeling frustrated," or "I'm frustrated."

- Go on a date to enjoy time with your partner and get some perspective on your relationship. Then when you're not in each other's faces and aren't talking about what's bothering you all day you can relax.

- Let each person write down their interactions and boundaries and then discuss them to see if they line up.

- Check-in with how you feel at regular intervals, e.g., after dinner, before going to bed, etc. This is the counterpart of "checking in" when you feel good and want to let your partner know how great he is (or she). Also, be sure to check in when you feel bad and can't stand it anymore.

- Sharing what is bothering you, not just attacking and blaming the other person for causing problems.

- If you're feeling drained, stressed out, or hopeless, ask your partner if he/she has noticed anything different about how you're acting. A partner may notice a different attitude, inward mood, or an untoward look in your eyes that bothers them (even if they don't know why). Sometimes self-disclosure is the key to repairing a relationship.

- If the problem is a constant pattern of things like arguing, fighting, or not listening, take a break from each other once in a while to give your relationship time to heal. Don't let the bad times rule your life, or you'll end up hating each other forever.

- Communicate feelings and needs. Sometimes each person can completely misunderstand the other's needs and desires and think that their partner does not love them anymore when the truth is something entirely different.

Functional and Relational Boundaries

Discipline is the process of establishing a clear distinction between the family's private and public spheres. This is also known as defining how much control a family member should have over the others. For example, defining how far a person can go in borrowing from their parent, mother, or father. A child would not want someone going through their phone and checking text messages because this would be an invasion of privacy; it would be disrespectful to both the parents and the child. Every child needs unconditional love, physical affection, and discipline to grow into an independent adult who can handle life on their own.

Withdrawal from boundaries

Criticizing someone's looks, body size, or clothing is a form of violence against an individual that causes hurt feelings. Just imagine a child constantly called fat, ugly, and stupid in front of their peers and not being able to take it anymore. This will cause the child to lash out eventually for no reason and not just to the criticizing individual.

Boundaries are a necessary part of the human experience. Whether physical, spiritual, or emotional, boundaries help us set limits and keep ourselves safe while opening up new levels of intimacy with those we love. It's important to establish boundaries before others cross them to maintain healthy relationships and respectful partnerships. But what if that boundary is drawn the wrong way? What if you've become so accustomed to living under someone else's boundaries that you end up performing self-abuse?

How do you know if it's time for some boundary maintenance? The first warning sign is when your negative thoughts about yourself outweigh your positive ones. When thoughts about being unlovable or unworthy become your default, you need to open up some serious lines of communication with yourself before you can truly begin to flourish in the way that you were meant.

The second warning sign is when those around you are not happy with relating to them. If it means upsetting loved ones, making demands on their time or energy, ignoring their needs and feelings, being dismissive and unkind in interactions. Does this sound familiar? It's about reconnecting with yourself and learning how to set healthy boundaries again.

Hostility against boundaries

This is when a child is hurt by his or her family and friends. They begin to feel as if no one loves or cares for them. They think that the only way to get that love and attention is through violence against another person.

Degradation of boundaries

This normally happens when a parent or close family member in the child's life abuses alcohol/drugs, physically, sexually, or verbally abuses them. This will cause the child to think as if they are less than what everyone else thinks of them.

Overcontrol

This is normally when parents over control their children. They cannot do anything without permission from their parents. When a child's parents are constantly nagging and criticizing them, they start to believe that no one wants them around because they always criticize them for every move they make in life.

Under control

This is when a child grows up and starts to think that no one is there to help them with problems or anything in general.

Lack of limits

This is where parents may see that no limits are being set on their children, causing them to harm another individual.

Hypocrisy

This usually happens when parents tell their children to obey their rules and boundaries but are criticized for not upholding them.

Not knowing the consequences

If parents do not teach their children, what would happen if they began acting out of love for themselves or what they did during their childhood? Most families that abuse their children have done so because of the consequences placed on them by other people.

Chapter 7:
Boundaries with Families and Friends

T hese are the people in our lives with whom we get to share ourselves, and it can feel like they know us better than anyone else. But they might not want them to know all the details of your life, and that's perfectly OK! Here are a few steps to help you create healthy boundaries with those around you.

First, review setting boundaries: having boundaries means setting limits on how much of your personal space someone gets or when you want them there. It's all about making sure that everyone has enough room. For example, you might its polite to someone when you ignore all their communication attempts. Maybe you don't want to answer their phone calls because it feels like you're spending more time on the phone than in the moment.

It's important to be aware of your thoughts and feelings and acknowledge when they pull you back. You don't have to act on your feelings (i.e., yelling at someone or asking them to leave), but you might choose to share how you're feeling. Setting boundaries is a good way of letting people know where you stand.

If having healthy boundaries doesn't feel right for you, you don't have to do it. Although it can be helpful in the long run, for your boundaries to be effective, they need to be informed by your true needs and desires. They should also come from a place of self-love and self-compassion.

When we set boundaries with others, we say that our time, ourselves, and our possessions belong. And even though most of us know that many of us don't act like it on some level! Let's talk about how having healthy boundaries might make you feel: setting boundaries might make you feel in charge of your life and allow you to say "no" when necessary.

Consider having each other time

When you say "yes" to someone, allow yourself to get pulled into their drama, or are willing to go above and beyond, this can be a form of giving of yourself. You're saying that their time is valuable. People will respect this and treat you accordingly. But when boundaries are broken (or ignored), it's because they don't think their time or yours is valuable - and they won't want to waste it with you!

What Needs You Share With Them

When you make a request or tell them that something you're doing is important to you, they may feel like you're rejecting them. This is because they share their time and experiences with the expectation that, in return, you will share yours as well. But it's important not to feel guilty when setting boundaries; it means that your time and experiences are ultimately about who you are. Setting boundaries doesn't mean you should feel like a jerk—it means owning your time and life.

How Reciprocal You Are

When you share your time and experiences with someone, it might make them feel like they own you. But again, this is a feeling that's not always true.

It's a common misconception that boundaries are about being self-centered and closed off. Yet, boundaries are more about how you interact with the world. For example, suppose you have a boundary of not speaking to certain people because of past disagreements. In that case, it's not a boundary if you get too close with no intention of initiating a conversation.

For example, you might think that talking on the phone three times a day is within your comfort zone. But, if you try it, you might find it's too much for you. Your limits may shift over time depending on your mood, stress levels, and the availability of support from others.

Sometimes people think they have no boundaries when so many become rigid and resistant to change. At the other extreme are the people who have few or no boundaries separating themselves from other people and situations. Your intent is key here because even though both extremes can be exhausting to navigate, one leads to freedom while the other contributes to a sense of lack of self or being trapped by circumstances.

One way to test your current level of boundaries is to ask yourself how you would feel if someone tried to cross your boundaries. Would you be shocked or resentful? If so, that's a good sign because it means you're not sure your boundary is correct.

168

How Much You Tell Them

It can be helpful to set boundaries in the way you share your thoughts and feelings. Be careful not to tell people things they may not want to know about (i.e., using the "too much information" excuse). It's important to keep some of these thoughts and feelings for yourself, or at least share them more appropriately with someone who wants to listen.

How You Treat Their Values

It's important to respect where your friends and family are coming from, but you don't have to agree with them all the time. For example, if you want to do something that goes against your parents' values (such as having sex, going to clubs, etc.), it might help you find someone to talk to about it. You don't have to tell your parents if you don't want to (maybe a school counselor or doctor). If you do tell your parents, it might help to share why you made this decision. It's important to let people know what's important to you, and not doing so might lead others to think that your time is up for grabs.

As a final example of having effective boundaries, let's talk about the subtle ways we communicate boundaries when we don't say "no." First, when you look at the situations below, see if you can identify what it means when someone says or does certain things.

How You Separate Your Emotions And Well-Being

For example, you might say you can't talk to someone because you're angry or upset about something. But if the other person can't help you

169

feel better, you consider that before deciding it would be better for both of you to give up the conversation. It's a good idea to know when to stop trying to solve someone else's problems. It might also help if you could separate your emotions and well-being from the person in question. Plus, it's important not to feel guilty for having these boundaries: they are part of who you are, it's okay to have them and important they are respected.

How You Affect Each Other's Lives

If you're not careful, being around certain people can make it more difficult to move forward in your life (like a friend who wants to talk about their problems all the time). For example, instead of just saying, "I don't want to talk about it," say, "I like talking with you, and I want our relationship to continue, but I don't want our conversations to affect my goals or well-being." Your boundaries are there for you: if someone doesn't respect them, that's okay.

How You Support Them

Depending on your relationship with someone, you may have to set boundaries in supporting them. If this gets in the way of your other obligations or well-being, it's okay to have a conversation with them and let them know how their problems affect you. For example, if the person sends incoherent emails at 2:00 am in the morning, you could say, "I like talking with you and helping when I can, but I need some time to rest and recharge. Can we talk tomorrow?"

Whether You're Able to Say "No"

One of the most important boundary issues is whether you're able to say "no", as it can cause long-term problems in your life. You might agree to do things that make you unhappy or uncomfortable or find yourself not getting enough rest because there are too many things going on. If this sounds like you, work on letting yourself say "no" - even if it's a little hard in the beginning. Don't feel bad if people get angry at you sometimes; apologize and decide how to deal with this situation the next time it comes up.

Chapter 8:
Boundaries in Dating

B oundaries can be related to meeting people, how often and for how long they can contact you, asking for your number, or what they're allowed to say in text messages. Think about the most important things that are nonnegotiable, and then fill in the gaps.

The next steps are to communicate those boundaries and stick with them when things inevitably go wrong. If someone wants your number or gets too pushy with their requests, try saying, "I only give my number out once I feel like we've had a decent conversation." This gives people a chance to back off, and it will affect your chances of them getting in contact if you want to keep the number.

Once you start getting into deeper conversations over the phone or meeting up with someone for coffee or drinks, it can be more difficult to manage your boundaries. I find that texting is a good way of holding onto our boundaries when we're uncertain and don't know what to expect from a conversation. A clear set of texting rules can be helpful here.

Just like in person, texting will only happen once things feel right and you feel comfortable enough to talk about more personal things. If we're enjoying each other's company over a good cup of coffee, that conversation shouldn't stop just because we stop drinking coffee.

I've learned that I'm happiest when I'm only talking to one person at a time, so watching out for the signs of someone who wants to be exclusive is a big part of staying happy in my relationships. I often tell him in person or over the phone, so there isn't any confusion about where we stand. This makes me feel more secure knowing that he respects me.

I know what you're thinking: "that sounds exhausting," and it can be. It's important to find the right balance between being open and honest with the people you're dating and having enough time to take care of yourself. If you feel like your life is slowly merging with your partner's, you can tell them that you need some space or a break in contact. I was excited when my boyfriend wanted to spend all his free time together, but after a few weeks of always being together, I started to lose interest.

When he noticed that I was pulling away, he started asking me how I felt about it. I explained to him that I wanted time with my best friend. At first, he was really surprised, but after reading up on the concept of "holding space" and a few more talks, he understood, and we haven't had a problem since.

Sometimes breaking away from each other for a while can be good for both people, but if you're trying to get back together and the person still doesn't respect your boundaries, they're probably not a match for you.

Why Dating?

The term "dating" as used by the church is not just a euphemism for something else. It refers to the dating done by non-married members of the church. The purpose of dating is to find someone who is a potential spouse. Dating should be seen as an opportunity for exploring and preparing for marriage; it is a time where you can discover a lot about yourself and those around you. It can be fun, educational, and mind-expanding. While going out with several people at once may seem like fun, it's not very effective at helping you decide who is right for you.

Emotional Boundaries You Should Set on The First Date

- Be respectful of each other and their time.
- Don't talk about things that aren't appropriate or may make someone uncomfortable or upset them.
- Don't talk about your past too much because it's not something you want to bring up to every date, but if you're going to be respectful and discreet at how you do it.
- Treat each other like your friends and not as a potential love interest, also. Don't get possessive of each other, especially in public!
- Don't be rude! This doesn't mean that you should be overly nice and try to make up for it by being mean and bugging people. Some politeness will get you further than being a total stranger.

- Don't rely on your date to pay for everything! If you know your relationship is going somewhere, pay at least your fair share of the expenses.
- Don't be friends with your date's friends while you're dating or friends of their family after getting together. If they're good people, respect their boundaries and don't be a burden.
- When you get a group of couples together, don't go around and ask people about their sex lives or any other personal questions.
- Don't have sex on the first date or any date until you're married, and don't have sex with anyone that isn't your spouse. It's just not worth it! It will only cause you to break up because you aren't meant for each other.
- Say YES to spending time together, whether it be going out for coffee or taking a walk through the park or whatever else may come up in your day while you're together, but say NO to anything against God's commandments or that degrades your relationship with Him.
- Don't text or call your date too often; it will make them think that you're too clingy and desperate for their attention.
- If your date is a close friend and they tell you something that makes you feel uncomfortable or mad, don't tell anyone else; take it up with the person who said it privately.
- If your date pays and you don't care for the person, don't try to do something nice for in return like seeing a movie or going out for food just as friends; be social with each other but set boundaries so that you don't get hurt later on if they break up with you.

- Don't pressure someone into being your date for the school dance or any other outing with many people you don't know. Sometimes it's best to end a friendship rather than suffer the pain caused by doing the things mentioned here

- Don't make everything about sex! If you're not comfortable telling someone that you're dating them, don't tell them, or if you want to, be diplomatic about it.

- If you're a single girl dating a guy, make sure he meets your parents! If you don't like someone, then fine, but don't have them around the house. You don't want to feel forced into doing something against God's commandments.

- Don't let the person you're dating think they can do whatever they want to you or treat you disrespectfully just because they are in a relationship with you.

- Don't try to force someone into relationship if it doesn't feel right! What's the point of being together if not for love and sexual involvement?

- Don't date someone if they are not willing to give you what you need. In short, don't just settle for anyone!

- If someone tries to hit on the person you're dating, tell them no politely and firmly! Don't be intimidated by person!

Chapter 9:
Boundaries on Marriage

M arriage is a partnership, one that requires two individuals to function and work together. It can be an amicable relationship where both parties share responsibilities and meet each other's needs. Or it can be more like a dictatorship, where the dominant spouse has all he controls and makes all the decisions.

Whatever kind of marriage you have, boundaries are important for maintaining healthy partnerships. Boundaries on marriage will allow you to maintain balance in your life while also staying married — just how you want it!

Here's how to set boundaries with your spouse:

1- Make sure both spouses are on board with setting boundaries.

2- Establish boundaries with your spouse that work. For example, "We're not going to argue." This is not an aggressive boundary; it's a cooperative boundary.

3- Understand that each boundary needs to be realistic and specific so you can both remember what the boundaries are. If you set a boundary too broad, then you can forget about it. If the boundary is too narrow and specific, it becomes useless because nothing bad happens when you don't follow it out of habit or convenience.

4- Communicate often to remind each other of the boundaries. Be clear about what your boundaries are and why they're important for maintaining a healthy partnership.

5- Have fun setting boundaries together!

Boundaries on marriage can be tricky, especially if you're unsure what the boundaries are or how to set them up. Knowing boundaries is very important because they allow your relationship to be safe and healthy. A relationship that has boundaries will be able to grow and be stronger.

Examples of common boundaries:

1) "I don't want to hear you talk about your ex." This boundary would mean that you would not want to hear your spouse talk about their past relationships, especially if things didn't work out well.

2) "We're not going to argue." This is a cooperative, amicable boundary; it means that you are both on the same page with how you feel about certain issues and choices.

3) "I need to talk about every decision we make." This boundary means your spouse will be open and honest with you when making decisions together. It's also a good way to prevent dictatorship in the relationship.

4) "We are not spending money without discussing it first." This boundary means that you will discuss money issues ahead of time because they are important parts of the relationship.

178

5) "I need to be heard at least once a week." This boundary allows you and your spouse to feel heard by each other regularly so you can have peace and move forward with your life (instead of feeling ignored, held back, or disconnected).

6) "I don't like you to have friends live with you." This boundary means that you are against letting your spouse have their friends move in; it's an issue of privacy and safety.

You can use these boundaries to create a healthy relationship with your spouse, so go ahead and set them up today!

TIPS ON HEALTHY MARRIAGE

Tip #1 — A marriage counselor can help

A marriage counselor can help you deal with many of your marriage struggles and help you communicate better with your spouse. You can find marriage counselors in a few different ways:

- Lookup "marriage counselor" near your address or zip code on Google
- Contact a local church and ask if they have marriage counselors on staff
- Explore online resources

Tip #2 — Hold onto your individuality

You can have the perfect marriage if you're willing to lose yourself. By doing this you may end up with a lot of problems in your marriage because you may not be meeting your spouse's needs and vice versa. To have a healthy marriage, it's important that both of you maintain your individuality and meet each other halfway, keeping your marriage healthy and strong.

Tip #3 — Don't let conflict lead to arguments

Conflict is normal in every relationship; it just means that the two individuals involved aren't on the same page. However, if you keep it going for a long time without resolving it, then the discord can become toxic in the relationship and cause problems.

Tip #4 — Let go of tired habits

Have you ever got yourself into the hot seat after being frustrated with your spouse and said something you regretted? It's good to let go of these habits because they will only negatively affect the marriage. For example, before discussing a problem with your spouse, think about whether or not you want to get into an argument. If so, it might be better to talk with them when you're not angry.

Tip #5 — Be selfish

Sometimes you have to be selfish to keep your marriage healthy. For example, if you're yelling at your spouse for being 10 minutes late, then they're going to be upset with you for being on their case. So instead of letting the argument escalate, take a few deep breaths and cool off.

Tip #6 — Make up who you are

If you're not happy with who you are in a marriage, why did you get married? It's important to realize that marriage changes your identity from an individual to a couple.

Tip #7 — Strive for balance

Both of you must talk about what the other person needs and then be willing to compromise.

Tip #8 — Argue fairly

In marriage, you must argue fairly. If a spouse is doing all of the talking or being disrespectful during an argument, they aren't being fair and are making it difficult for both spouses to communicate effectively.

Tip #9 — Find a time and place for your monologues

Sometimes you need to talk out a problem or a disagreement by yourself to express your feelings healthily.

Tip #10 — Tackle threats aggressively

When you and your spouse conflict, think about what they're saying and also about how they're saying it. You both must take action to protect the relationship. So if your spouse is threatening to leave the relationship, consider what they're saying and find ways to deal with the threat.

Tip #11 — Stay in touch with your friends

You must maintain your individuality in marriage. Maintain your friendships with other people and avoid becoming isolated. You're still a person, so you have to stay connected with people.

Tip #12 — Disagreements are normal

Sometimes it's going to be difficult for two spouses to agree on everything. However, both must try their best not to get upset or frustrated about it. It's healthy for disagreements and different viewpoints to exist as long as both parties can communicate their feelings effectively and find a resolution.

Tip #13 — Enjoy each other

You must enjoy your spouse for who they are, even if you don't always agree with them. You need to be able to experience the good things about your partner without getting obsessive or critical in any way.

Tip #14 — Talk honestly about your feelings and skills

For example, if one of you is having difficulty doing something at home or work, that person can provide the other with feedback to improve their performance.

Tip #15 — Be careful how you give advice

When you're in a relationship, you may find that the other person is giving you advice. But make sure you're reasonably taking this advice. Don't try to implement all their suggestions at once. Also, be careful about what kind of advice they're giving. If they're expecting you to do everything perfectly, they need to recognize that will never happen and so help them develop more realistic expectations.

Tip #16 — Avoid telling jokes or asking personal questions

They might think that you're checking upon them, which could be very frustrating for both of you.

Tip #17 — Don't Be shallow or jealous

It's not okay to express your jealousy by criticizing the people dating your partner's ex-partner. This behavior is shallow and can make it difficult for your relationship to grow in the right direction. If you feel insecure about the other person being with someone else, talk about it instead of expressing negative feelings by joking around with your partner.

Tip #18 — Don't be passive aggressive

Passive-aggressive behavior can be very frustrating for a partner. It might seem like your partner has done something wrong, but they haven't made any obvious mistakes.

Tip #19 — Don't insult your partner with hypocritical statements

Your partner might feel hurt by your comments if you associate them with their family or ancestry. Either way, this behavior will make them feel like nobody likes them and that they're not worthy of being loved by someone else.

It's a mental health issue that affects all of us at some point in our lives. It's common for those of us who have experienced it not to identify it as such. Unfortunately, it can also be a symptom of other presenting conditions such as anxiety, depression, PTSD, and addiction. It may be a coincidence that those diagnosed with these other conditions also struggle with this problem.

It's hard even to begin to talk about this because we all know people who are so clearly affected by narcissistic tendencies that they're not worth the bother of understanding.

Chapter 10:
Boundaries with Spouses and Children

W hen it comes to our families, they dictate the expectations we have for one another and how we expect each other to behave. Sometimes these boundaries are clear, but sometimes they're not.

You don't get along with your father-in-law? It's pretty easy to know that this relationship is unhealthy and you need to limit your time with him. But what about a parent who expects his 45-year-old daughter (who still lives at home) to drop everything for him whenever he wants? This is often a difficult boundary to enforce because family members are quick to say, "You're all I've got!" when boundaries are set.

Most people are forced to make their own decisions. We either decide that we won't allow certain behavior or decide that we're the adult in the family, and we'll make that decision on our own. But what happens when our parents, brothers, sisters, aunts, uncles, and cousins don't follow these rules?

It's not uncommon to feel like we need to protect children from their grandparents because they're different than us or just for no good reason at all. We put younger children in time-outs or refuse to play with them whenever they come over because their behavior isn't "good enough" for us.

Boundaries with Spouses

It's virtually impossible to have a peaceful marriage if one partner will not respect others' boundaries. A conflict-free marriage requires two people who hear what the other is saying and respond respectfully without feeling like their self-worth is being threatened or judged.

In any relationship, if one person has all of the power and control, you create a dynamic where the other person has to manipulate and deceive to get their needs met. This is unfair to the other person; it puts undue pressure on the one in control and can cause them to lose sight of their own needs.

It's impossible to be well-adjusted when going through the developmental stages of life (childhood, adolescence, young adulthood). We are born into a family with parents who have different expectations than our own which creates internal conflict that plays itself out in different ways as we leave our teens and enter adulthood.

In an article titled "A Parent's Guide to Raising Emotionally Healthy Adult Children," the author points out that parents should not try to change their child's behavior but rather help them find their reasons and motivations for changing. When I was growing up, I used humor and manipulation to get my parents to stop nagging me about studying. In retrospect, I wasn't interested in studying and would have ignored them even if they had stopped nagging.

This is one of the many reasons why boundaries are so important in a marriage. When you have clear, defined boundaries, you don't have to tell your mate what to do or how to behave because they already

186

know. Having a mature and well-adjusted partner allows each person to be themselves, creating a more peaceful and loving atmosphere within the relationship.

No one likes being caught in the middle of his/her parents' battles. The child always feels like it's their fault. In reality, it's the responsibility of the adults to live up to their roles as parents.

Boundaries With Children

• Respect their boundaries from the beginning, so they know what's acceptable and not acceptable in their life. The parents of a new baby must agree on boundaries before the birth, as it sets the tone for all future events and decisions during childhood (such as sleepovers).

• If your child wants to spend time with an adult, it's okay. They won't automatically be labeled as bad. If a mother doesn't let her daughter spend time with a friend, in the end, she will have a bitter teenager. A relationship with an adult is supposed to be healthy and safe.

• If your son is leaving the house to visit a friend, reassure him that it's not a bad thing to hhave friends. If he needs to be alone, he can go somewhere else too (the library or school).

• I always feel bad asking my children to get dressed for church or a special event if they don't want to. I have an agreement with my kids that I will only pay for their activities if they are actively participating in them. If they aren't interested, then it's not fair to ask me to pay out of my abundance.

• Children should be taken to church at least a couple of times each month; help them make plans, if necessary.

• If your teenage son is rambunctious, understand that he needs time to process his thoughts. Being concerned about him may be an effective way to help him work through his problems. Encourage him to talk, play sports, and engage in other typical teenage activities.

• Children need boundaries the same as adults do. If you have a particular boundary that you have set with your child...then enforce it.

Boundaries with Loved Ones

Start off by working from the inside out. Learn how you want your loved ones to treat you and then see how they respond to your requests and boundaries. If it's something that makes you uncomfortable, don't be afraid to say, no. Avoid hinting at a boundary without addressing the real issue. You might not get what you asked for, but ultimately everyone ends up happier and more accepting because the issue was discussed and worked out rather than ignored (which can result in resentment).

Setting Boundaries

Value yourself and your time

When your time is valued, no one's time is wasted, and others will respect you. To help increase you self-worth, be clear in your views. Often it is not what is being done to us, but rather how we react and respond to the situation. For example, a man might want his wife, daughter, or mother to take care of dinner every night. However, she might see this request as unreasonable and insist he do it himself. The underlying issue is that his wife does not value him (an example of what we often call "non-self-love").

Permit yourself to do what's best for you

If you're unsure what your best course of action is, ask a trusted friend or family member for their honest feedback. Do not blame yourself for the results of bad behavior. If a situation does not go well, learn from it and move on. Remember to be forgiving and understanding with yourself as well.

Have the courage to say no

Saying no can feel scary, especially when someone asks you to do something that would be very difficult or uncomfortable for you, such as interacting with a person who has been unfriendly or going to a place where others make comments about your appearance, etc.

Know your triggers and anticipate them. Anticipate the times you might be triggered, such as a breakup, a birthday, the holidays, an anniversary of abuse, or other trauma. If you know your triggers, you can prepare yourself to avoid them by doing something else, such as listening to music or taking a walk.

If it's not worth the risk, then don't do it. Do not hang out with people who make you feel uncomfortable. Don't wait too long to let go of toxic relationships or situations because they take over your life and begin to control you.

Be clear about your needs and communicate them

When you learn to communicate your needs, you are more likely to get what you want. Your needs are important and not going away. Find other people who enjoy spending time with you and compliment them. Give them compliments too! It will make them feel good, and they will want to spend more time with you, so everyone wins!

Practice saying no

The first few times you say no might feel awkward but stick with it, and you will get used to it. Set limits on time spent with friends, family, coworkers, and others. Allowing others to use your time without setting limits can cause problems in relationships. Be sure your self-respect is not jeopardized by allowing others to be disrespectful of your time.

If you are experiencing difficulties at work or school, talk with someone about how you feel instead of worrying about it alone. You don't need to go into the details; explain that something is bothering you and leave the rest up to them to help decide what steps should be taken next.

Make a list of coping strategies

Brainstorm with friends and family members to come up with ideas for coping with difficult situations. As long as you don't tell anyone else what to do, you will be able to work through things on your own and learn what works best. Trust your instincts, even if they are difficult to follow at first.

If someone asks you out or wants to spend time with you, it is a good idea to ask a friend or family member for feedback. You should also ask yourself: would I want someone close to me to be doing this? Otherwise, don't do it.

Chapter 11:
Boundaries with Others

B oundaries are rules or limits people put on themselves when they interact with others. We establish boundaries to protect ourselves and set the tone of our relationships. Our boundaries can be physical, sexual, emotional, intellectual, and verbal.

Communication with other people is a way of talking about what we need in terms of respect, attention, help, and more. It's important for people to have boundaries and not let other people walk all over them. I don't like to play games or hurt other people, but I'd rather say something directly and be honest about my feelings than keep quiet to avoid conflict. This way, I feel more comfortable with myself, which makes me a happier person.

Boundaries help make us feel in control of our lives. They are rules that give us guidelines for interacting with others; they let us know what is okay and how we want to be treated. We can establish our boundaries and change them over time. Most importantly, boundaries help us define who we are.

Boundaries help us set limits on behavior or what we allow other people to do. Boundaries also show other people how far they may go in their actions and words toward us. They give us an idea of what is acceptable for ourselves and others, as well as the limits of our rights.

TIPS TO CREATE HEALTHY BOUNDARIES WITH OTHERS

Verbal violations

Verbal violations are the most common ways to get our needs met. People often say and do hurtful things without realizing it. So be alert to how your words affect others. If someone tells you to do something you don't feel comfortable doing, like touch them or have sex with them, say "no" and then explain why you don't want to do it.

Verbal violations can be verbal threats, name-calling, put-downs, insulting jokes, and so forth. If you hear something hurtful or mean coming from someone else, say something to the person. It could be hard because most people don't know how to deal with someone who is being honest. But if you let people control your life verbally and not have boundaries when people are hurtful, it hurts other people and yourself in the long run.

Psychological and emotional boundary violations

Sometimes people test our boundaries by doing inappropriate things, like "bumping heads" with us. They laugh at the wrong times and make insensitive jokes. They try to talk you into doing things you don't want to do. These are usually thoughtless acts on the part of the perpetrator and not intentionally malicious.

It's best to try to look at these situations as learning experiences. Remember how it felt when someone did this to you in the past and understand why they are doing it now. When someone tests your boundaries, they are looking for an outlet for their own emotions or

193

an easy way out of a situation they don't feel comfortable with. But if you let people control your emotions by accepting what they say and do, it hurts you.

Physical boundary violations

Physical boundary violations are the most common type of abuse in relationships. These can include forms of physical force, like hitting, grabbing, pinching, choking, sexual contact without consent such as rape and sexual harassment, verbal threats like yelling at someone in an angry voice, or "putting words in their mouth" by misrepresenting something that happened between you two. Physical abuse also includes non-verbal forms of aggression like ignoring someone, not speaking to them, not caring about them, or making fun of them.

Boundary violations may involve either physical or psychological harm or both. Abusers use physical means and may also use sexual coercion and other threats to control their victims. In some cases, psychological abuse can be the most damaging form of domestic violence, especially when it is chronic. An abuser's power over a victim can be greatly increased if the abuser knows how to play on their victim's fears, insecurities, and self-doubts.

Know thyself

Know your self-image, strengths, and weaknesses. Learn as much you can say about who you are as a person, and when you know yourself, you will be able to respect yourself. Be proud of who you are, but also be aware of what is wrong with yourself. Be honest and truthful with others about who you are and get to know them too. If anything in the relationship doesn't seem right or feels off, speak up immediately and don't let anyone violate your boundaries by blaming it on your imagination. If something feels wrong for someone else, then it's probably wrong for everyone involved.

Take responsibility for yourself

You are supposed to be responsible for yourself, but if you let others control your life and not have boundaries, no one will respect you. The worst thing is that you won't respect yourself either. Make it a point to do things that are personally important and schedule them every day. Create a life where you get to do what makes you happy and feel good when other people aren't controlling what you do. Create a life where you don't feel resentful towards yourself and others because you are doing something right and they are doing something wrong. Don't keep yourself down by blaming other people for what they do. It is not their fault that you are depressed or unhappy with your life.

Develop a healthy respect for yourself

If you have a healthy respect for yourself, you will know that you are your own person and deserve to be treated as such. Suppose other people don't respect your boundaries and violate them regularly. In that case, it may be time to re-evaluate who is in your life and the quality of those relationships.

Heed the warning signs

When you notice signs that your life is becoming unmanageable and you can't seem to move forward, it is time for a change. Many people don't know when they are in a rut and going down a path that leads to depression because they have never been through it before. They think that depression is something that only other people experience, and they put their heads in the sand and pretend that nothing is wrong. You cannot ignore the pain of emotional abuse or neglect just because you want to; it will creep up if you do.

It's critical to take the time to listen to your inner voice. If you find yourself feeling angry, withdrawn, and constantly giving up your needs for others, you might have a boundary problem. You need to set limits with those who talk over you or make demands that you cannot meet. Finding your boundaries will help release pent-up anger and frustration. Also, it will show people that they cannot mistreat or abuse you without consequences.

But don't forget about setting boundaries with yourself. It's important to take care of your needs and not do things that will only hurt you. If you want something out of your reach, you probably will never get it. If you know you are being taken advantage of, then stand up for yourself by saying no. Letting others get their way just because they want something signifies that your boundaries are not defined.

Don't try to fix people

Sometimes, we feel that we need to fix people. Maybe someone has hurt us, or maybe they have said they want to change but never do.

We can't force anyone to change, and we shouldn't try to make them change because it will drive us crazy. You need to change what you can control, and let go of the things you cannot control as part of that process.

If someone doesn't want help, then don't make them feel bad for not wanting it. Be there when they are ready to accept your help, but don't try to force them into your mold and become the person you think they should be. Allowing someone to be who they are means accepting them exactly as they are. Don't morph them into something they are not.

You are in charge of your choices

Don't try to be what you are not. If you let the old rules and who you thought you were determine your actions today, it will become a self-fulfilling prophecy that doesn't work. Your destiny is in your hands. You are powerful and in control of what happens next! If you feel like it is time to leave a relationship, create a plan that allows it to happen. No one else can stand in the way of your happiness, and you have every right to be happy!

Separate yourself from others

When you let someone else's problems become your own, you may wind up feeling very emotionally drained and depressed. You need to have your own life separate from the lives of anyone else involved in your life. It may seem strange because we all think that sharing our lives with someone is a good thing, but if their lives don't work with yours, it isn't worth it.

If you are trying to take care of someone else or be there for them all the time, then they have become too much of a focal point in your life. Ask for help. You are not the last person in your life to love. Find the people in your life who truly make a difference and use them as a resource for extra support when needed. Remove someone from your life if they are causing you pain, and make sure there is someone else waiting to fill their shoes.

Redefine your relationship

Your relationships are an important part of who you are. When a relationship is toxic, it can leave you feeling miserable and alone. If you are willing to redefine your relationships, then most problems can be resolved to work for everyone involved. If you can't communicate with someone, it is a sign of insecurity because they don't respect themselves.

Whether it's family, friends, or a group of people who can relate to your situation, there is nothing wrong with talking out your problems and their relationship to boundaries. You may or may not be ready to take action, but talking things out is a good way to understand what still needs to be done.

And when you are ready to take action, you will hear from other people who have gone down the same path how they came up with a solution that worked well.

Chapter 12:
How to Create Effective Boundaries

T o create effective boundaries, it's important first to understand your feelings. Do you feel angry? Frustrated? Resentful? Sad? Unsure about how you feel? Once you've named your emotions, remind yourself that your feelings are valid - they don't have to make sense or be consistent with what others think. Whatever you're feeling is A-okay. Setting boundaries is not selfish, as many people believe.

Ways to Create and Preserve Boundaries

There are several ways to create boundaries in your life. The method you choose is the one that works best for you.

Name your limits

You have the right to choose how you want to be treated, and there are ways of communicating those choices. First, it's important to say what you mean. Instead of using vague words like "a little," try using specific words like, "I would prefer it if you didn't [fill in the blank]."

Second, there are times when it's an effective idea to use "no" – as long as you're choosing your limits and not allowing other people's expectations to influence your life.

Setting boundaries in relationships with children, family members, or your spouse is a difficult task. It's even more difficult when you remember that you're responsible for your child and the adults in their life. And remember, you're also responsible for yourself!

Start by making a list of the things you would like to change in your life. It's important to notice when people try to get away with doing things that bother you, so jot down these moments. For example, if someone tries to make an appointment at a time when they know you can't attend, write it down. Or, if someone consistently ignores your requests or fails to do what they've promised, write it down as this could be passive-aggressive behavior on their part, so watch out for these moments.

Tune into your feelings

Because we make ourselves angry or sad when we feel violent or scared, it's helpful to note these moments so you can recognize them. Experiencing any emotional pain signals that something in your life isn't as you'd like it to be. In most cases, this pain points to something that doesn't feel good. Is there a relationship problem that needs fixing? Could you rather have more personal time? Perhaps someone is expecting too much from you or taking advantage of your kindness or generosity.

Ask yourself whether any of these situations are creating feelings of anger, sadness, fear, etc. If so, make a list of the things that are causing this pain in your life. Then, start writing down ideas for change. Next, imagine how you want these situations to be, and then write down a few ways to make those changes happen.

For example, let's say you're tired of being on the phone with a pushy salesperson who won't take no for an answer. Maybe the salesperson can send you information about their products in the mail or email it to you so if you're interested, you have time to look it over before making a decision.

Be direct

Say what you mean clearly and directly. Once you've named your limits, have a conversation with the other person. Explain that having conversations like these is part of your relationship rules. For example, if you're tired of being interrupted or feeling like other people don't take you seriously when you talk, this is important information to share with those around you. Tell them it's part of your life choices.

Don't allow others to pressure or guilt trip you into changing your mind about how things will be in your relationships. And, if they try, explain that this is a boundary you chose for yourself.

Rehearse the conversation ahead of time if it makes it easier. You might even choose a time when both of you are calm and have some privacy, so there aren't interruptions. This will help you feel more focused on speaking your truth versus being distracted by other things, like being nervous about the outcome.

Be prepared for resistance. It's very common to experience anger from the person you have this conversation with. What's important is that you express your feelings and explain why this is an important issue to resolve.

Give yourself permission

If others continue to pressure you, suggest they stop it. They might tell you they feel hurt and confused when you don't let them know how things are going in your life and understand your perspective. If people insist, explain that you have not changed your mind about what's best for you; this is still part of how things will be between you.

Sometimes you might need to make these rules clear if they are not respected. If people don't respect your limits, it's up to you whether you want to continue the relationship. And, if you need to leave, do so. This is a difficult situation, but at some point, it's up to you to decide if being stressed out and angry is worth it.

Practice self-awareness

Be mindful of any feelings that arise in these situations. Is there anger? Frustration? Sadness? Do you feel hurt that people don't listen to you? These all signs that you might be feeling something other than what you're experiencing. So, ask yourself if the situation is making you feel this way or if it's coming from inside of you. If it's coming from inside, what is it telling you about your life?

If the situation has made you angry or upset, take a few moments to acknowledge these feelings and breathe into them like a wave on the oceanfront. This is an opportunity to let these feelings out so they don't build up and poison your relationships. How well you can handle these feelings is a sign of your strength.

Be open-minded about learning from your experiences. You need to take the time to review what has happened during each situation that's brought up feelings of anger, sadness, or hurt in the past. Did you listen to yourself? Did you trust your instincts? Or did you rely on another person's point of view? By taking the time to review, things can become clearer and help in future conversations where similar things might arise.

<u>Consider your past and present</u>

Often, feelings of anger, sadness, or hurt in our past can influence how we feel and behave today. We might not consciously realize that they have affected us for years, but it doesn't mean that the feelings don't exist.

The more aware you are of what has made you feel this way, the more likely you'll be able to find a way to make progress in these situations. Think back on specific interactions from the past and those moments whem you felt this way. You might not remember what happened, but sometimes these experiences can come back if we are open enough to receive them.

What do I want out of life?

When you have feelings of anger, sadness, or hurt, you are blocked from everyone else and the world. To move forward, it is important to open up to new experiences. You want more for yourself than to stay stuck in the same old patterns, and doing this will give you what you need to enjoy a healthier and happier future. Start by listing all the things in life that make you happy.

Make self-care a priority

When you are not feeling good about yourself, it can be hard to care for yourself. However, this is key to maintaining your self-esteem.

Elias says: "We all know what helps us feel better in general, such as laughter or hugs from friends and family, but sometimes we may need some extra help to get out of a rut. This is especially true when we can suffer through seasonally affected depression (SAD) or just be caught in a bit of a funk. While you might not have control over exactly what life throws at you, there are plenty of ways to boost your mood and get your mind out of the doldrums when you're feeling low."

Catch yourself in the moments when you're thinking negatively about yourself or someone else. When you start to feel down, remind yourself that you're going through a hard time, and that's okay. Let the negative thoughts come into your mind, but don't hold onto them for too long.

Bringing back your positive thoughts instead of continually dwelling on the negative ones will help bring those negative thoughts back down to a manageable level.

Seek support

You might even want to consider a counselor who specializes in relationships and relationship issues. If a counselor is what you're looking for, try finding a local therapist through the American Counseling Association (ACA). You can find therapists' profiles on their website, or click here to search for a counselor in your area. They don't have fees or insurance requirements, so either way, it's usually pretty affordable.

Talk about it. The more you talk about your thoughts and feelings, the better you will feel about yourself and your life. Indeed, many of the situations that could be driving your emotions are not likely to change; but at least talking about them helps you process the emotions they have caused in you, which should help free up some of that energy, so it's not directed back onto yourself. You can ask your family to allow you to talk about these things when you feel overwhelmed or disconnected from them.

Be assertive

Take control of your emotional life. Learn to stand up for yourself and what you want. We've all been in situations where we feel stuck in a negative place, and that's okay. We just need to be aware that this is coming up for us, and it's going to take time to get out of it. It might be something that happened recently, or maybe you've been struggling with this feeling for a while now — but the key is learning how to recognize those feelings and bring them into your awareness. And once they're there, you'll have the opportunity to take control of them rather than letting them control you.

Start small

Don't rush into big changes all at once. Take one step at a time, and then look back and evaluate how it's going for you. There are a lot of things you can do to help yourself feel better, so take your time in making them happen.

Be persistent

Don't give up on yourself, even if the first few steps don't get you anywhere. Just keep trying and eventually, you will find what works for you. This includes when it comes to changing your emotional reactions by watching those responses more closely. When we don't stop being aware of these reactions, we can learn to notice their triggers quicker than before and identify the strategies that work best to manage them.

Chapter 13:
Being Assertive

E veryone always says that you should be assertive, often with the implication that people who are not assertive are "passive" or "submissive." But what does it mean to be assertive?

First, we need to define the word. Assertiveness means giving yourself a voice without jeopardizing someone else's voice. It means making your needs and wants to be known in a way that is both clear and respectful of other people's needs and wants. It means not getting off on other people's needs or wants. It means not allowing others to get off on your needs or wants. It means that you don't care if you lose friends, lovers, family members, and friends over a boundary violation.

In a nutshell, assertiveness is about having respect for yourself and respecting others at the same time. This attitude works in all areas of your life—from how you communicate with your boss to how you dress to conduct yourself in personal relationships and sexual encounters.

Assertive Communication

Assertive communication is a form of interpersonal communication that seeks to avoid conflict by expressing and respecting personal boundaries. Staying assertive is not easy. It's worth the time and effort because assertiveness creates healthy relationships while aggression usually destroys them. Assertiveness is an important strategy for workplace harmony, relationship success, and personal peace of mind.

Being assertive has a lot to do with being in control of how you want others to behave around now and later in your life. You can't always control what others say or how they act, but you can control how you react to those behaviors.

There are two components to staying assertive in relationships. There is the external component of how you behave (your behavior) and the internal component of how you respond to behavior (your emotions).

The outer part of staying assertive has a lot to do with keeping your calm, remaining focused on your goals, seeing the situation in a positive light, handling surprises calmly, and keeping yourself out of "fight or flight" mode. The internal part of staying assertive has more to do with controlling your thoughts and feelings so they don't take over your actions. You want to maintain as much control as possible to think clearly and act appropriately.

Passive Behavior

Passive behavior is characterized by an avoidance of a situation, a delay in confrontation, or a lack of assertion. When you act passively, you may not express your feelings and opinions even when you know those feelings and opinions are valid. Passive behavior is a way to spare yourself the anxiety and discomfort of speaking up. It may also result in losing your voice, losing others' respect, and even losing friends.

While passive behavior may be a means to an end, it isn't always the best way to achieve those ends. Being passive often causes more problems than it solves and keeps you from solving them. In many cases, passive behavior may be a symptom of the problems addressed.

Passive behavior can also involve making excuses for other people's bad behavior to avoid conflict. Sometimes, this passive behavior may be accompanied by aggressive or passive-aggressive behaviors that come out as the situation escalates. Passive behavior is often used in workplace politics and relationships to gain control over others without being aggressive.

Aggressive Behavior

Aggressive behavior is characterized by expressing one's feelings or opinions in a direct and hostile manner. Aggression is often used as a way to get others to respond, listen or submit. The use of aggression can be very effective in getting the attention you want, but it can escalate into violence, leading to life-altering consequences. Aggressive behavior is often accompanied by passive behavior in an attempt to control others.

When people feel that they are not being heard or respected, they may become very aggressive. They may say and do everything within their power to defeat the person who is causing them stress or discomfort. Usually, people will resort to passive or aggressive behavior to control the situation and the other person.

Surprising or abrupt behavior is a form of aggression characterized by sudden and unexpected behavior meant to alter the other person's environment. When you act surprisingly or abruptly, you will likely create shock in the other person's body language, facial expressions (eyes), and verbal communication (tone).

Passive-Aggressive Behavior

Passive-aggressive behavior is an emotional behavior characterized by indirect or covert hostility. Passive-aggressive behavior is usually intended to harass, damage, or harm someone. Still, it can also be used as a means of self-protection in situations where you cannot express yourself directly. It usually consists of an indirect or indirect expression of hostility through "underhanded" tactics. It is often characterized by the use of sarcasm, hostility, resistance, and obstructionism to get people to do what you want them to do.

The use of passive-aggressive behavior can be very effective in getting people to do what you want them to do, but there's always a chance that it will backfire on you in a big way. Passive aggression can be especially difficult to deal with because it often involves deception and guilt. The person might say one thing while they mean something else. Such behavior can also help people cover up their true feelings from others, even if they are unhappy with those feelings.

What are the Benefits of Being Assertive?

There are many benefits to being assertive. Assertiveness can help you to get ahead in your career. Assertiveness can help you to create better relationships. Being assertive can help you achieve the goals you have set for yourself, and in doing so, it can increase your self-esteem and sense of self-worth.

Being an assertive person will not solve all of your problems or make every situation perfect, but it will give you a greater sense of control over your surroundings and over your own life. In many cases, being assertive may make life easier by creating the circumstances and situations you want to live the way you want.

Assertiveness could also prevent misunderstandings or hurt feelings. Being assertive may also make you feel better about yourself because it shows others that you respect yourself, which will make them respect you more. Being more assertive can also help you to stop being passive or aggressive. Passive behavior can be destructive and sometimes even life-threatening.

How to be More Assertive

There's no magic formula for assertiveness, but there are some basics that you should know. This is important that will help you to become more assertive. Listen and respond appropriately when people talk, even if this doesn't seem like the right time or place to respond.

Learning to be Assertive

Many people learn how to be assertive by reading books and taking quizzes and tests. Some people even learn how to be more assertive by watching videos and participating in webinars with guidance from a professional or a group of peers. Whatever method is chosen, an individual will need to practice being assertive in different situations to become second nature.

Identifying the problem is the first step in becoming more assertive. Identifying when and where your problem may occur will create an opportunity to take anticipatory action. This is a way of planning how you will respond to certain situations before they happen. By using the information gained from this step, individuals can monitor their behavior and begin to make changes as they are able.

Becoming more assertive helps individuals build positive relationships with peers, family members, friends, and coworkers. It may be beneficial because project confidence is a valuable skill that many people look for when hiring someone for a job or dealing with potential clients.

Chapter 14:
Boundaries with People Who Use You

P airing empathy with boundaries is a delicate balance. It's important to help people who abuse and control you, but it's also important to take care of yourself. If you continue to give someone your time, energy, money, and love when they don't respect or reciprocate that in return, you're putting yourself at risk for more harm.

So how do we find this balance? You may need to spend some time understanding the difference between selfless service for the sake of others vs. supporting others from a place of compassion.

Person "A"

These people talk about their problems, then expect a friend to solve them. For the sake of privacy, I'll call this person "A." It's not that they're looking for sympathy or want pity - they want help. But just because A wants help doesn't mean they deserve it. I believe that almost all people who use others are needy, and they're dependent on relationships. They enter into intimate, personal, and even sexual relationships to feel less lonely. And because people use them, they often don't have a clear understanding of their needs or how to meet them.

What I've seen over the years is that when A finally gets serious about finding relief from their problems by getting help, most people they've used will find an excuse to punish A for being "too needy" or "being manipulative". Then, I've seen people that use A get mad at A for not supplying enough help. These are unfortunate dynamics and heavy addictions.

A needs to start asking themselves why they don't have clearer boundaries with all the people they use. When someone uses them, that's when they're vulnerable, messy, and in need of help on an intimate level. They want help to meet their own needs and have been deceived into believing the relationship is personal or sexual when it's not.

People use others for many reasons:

They're lonely and desperate for human connection: People use others because they don't know how to meet their own emotional needs or have a proper sense of self-esteem. They don't know how to create healthy relationships, and they only know how to use people.

They can't set boundaries: I've also heard people say they're afraid of looking like a jerk if they set boundaries. If someone doesn't feel like they're worthy of self-respect, they'll depend on others and won't feel entitled to it for themselves.

They're passive-aggressive and believe in taking advantage: There's nothing more sadistic than passive-aggressive behavior. And it's a way that some people use others. They will use them for help and then sabotage them to feel better about themselves because they're in pain.

They're emotional vampires: Some people are energetic vampires who only see others as food sources for their own emotional needs. These people are addicted to being used by others and want to feed on their pain or drama. They're so addicted to this "emotional crack" they'll take advantage of anyone or anything that they see as a potential supply of energy or sadness - even if it's an object. It can be like watching rom-coms, reading erotic fan fiction, or writing stories online about how bad life is.

They have a narcissistic disorder: Someone who has a narcissistic personality disorder believes that all of their needs, wants, and desires are more important than others. As a result, they can't respect other people's boundaries and invade everyone else's space to satisfy their needs.

If you want to meet your spiritual and emotional needs in healthy ways, don't try to meet them in unhealthy ways. Don't try to meet them dynamically or compulsively. Don't try to meet your emotional needs by changing people into something they're not - their problems aren't yours - you're not responsible for how they feel or think about themselves. Don't try to meet your emotional needs by using other people. And don't try to meet your emotional needs by using drugs or alcohol.

Ways to Set Boundaries With Narcissistic People

If you're in a relationship with someone who has a narcissistic personality disorder, it's important to set boundaries because they won't respect them. Remember that narcissists don't have a sense of self-respect, they only know how to use people, and they're unable to create healthy intimate relationships.

If you want support for dealing with someone who can't respect boundaries, then it's important to find appropriate support for yourself. You have options:

1. Support groups: Narcissistic Abuse Support is an online support group, and they also have a private Facebook page.

2. Counselors: Talk to your family doctor or spiritual counselor about getting a referral for individual counseling to help you deal with this issue.

3. Self-help books: They all address how to set healthy boundaries with a narcissistic personality disorder or behave similarly.

If you are feeling hopeless, don't try to solve it alone. Please seek professional therapy and support from those who can help you heal, especially if you're dealing with a narcissistic family member.

Chapter 15:
Boundaries and Self Esteem

S elf-esteem can significantly affect how a person views their world and others around them. When someone feels stressed or anxious, it's easy for them to believe that there is nothing they can do about it. They feel like they are not in control of their own life. This can lead to a very negative perspective on life and may result in the belief that nothing is worth striving for. They may feel helpless, which can be further reinforced by their fears and beliefs that they are not worthy of being happy.

People need to recognize that they have self-esteem it's perfectly normal to experience feelings of sadness or anxiety, even when facing challenging situations. Taking a look at your own beliefs about life can help you gain more control over your challenges, which will increase your self-esteem.

Boundaries can help a person gain personal control as their self-esteem increases. People who feel powerless have no control over their own lives and are at the mercy of others. When a person is in this position, it's important to recognize that they have a voice and can make informed choices. Even if they are not always in control, this can become the case when they face challenges that involve self-esteem or confidence.

Taking personal responsibility and acting responsibly in certain situations can help gain a person's greater self-esteem. It's important

217

to recognize that these skills will be difficult to learn. Regardless, he or she cannot change everything about their life. Personal boundaries can help a person to take control of their own lives and improve their self-esteem.

Self-esteem

A vital part of healthy relationships and finding the right partner depends on it. If you are going out with someone you do not seem to trust, you should probably think about your relationship again. Self-esteem also helps people cope with life because it gives them something positive to live for. It teaches them about how strong they are and how much control they have over their own lives.

Self-esteem is not something a person will just automatically have. It must be worked on intentionally and can take some time to get to where you want it. Learning to say, no, when you do not want to do something will make it easier for you to say, yes, when it's more important to take care of yourself.

This can be especially true if you have a high-pressure job or try to fit too much into your schedule. You should try not to let your work life crowd out the important parts of your personal life and neglect the important people in your life as you focus on work. A combination of the two is ideal, but it may take some sacrifices on your part to get there.

Remember that communication is key. When you can discuss your partner's issues openly and honestly, you can work things out with respect for each other.

A healthy relationship with self-esteem

Partners who develop a healthy relationship with self-esteem can communicate their needs and feelings to each other. They can accept a partner's transgressions without having negative reactions that may cause the relationship to deteriorate. This is especially important if there are conflicts or disagreements about something that has happened in the past.

Healthy relationships with self-esteem are built on mutual respect between partners, and both people feel good about themselves and their relationship. They can talk things out when there are differences of opinion and find resolutions that make them feel better about themselves and their partner.

People who have healthy relationships with self-esteem believe in themselves enough that they don't need validation from others all of the time. They have goals and a direction in life that makes them feel good about their future. They choose partners who respect them and make them happy.

To begin a healthy relationship with self-esteem, it is important to set goals for manageable yourself. Make a list of things you want to accomplish in your life and decide how you can reach those goals. If you have financial worries or other things that are holding you back from achieving those goals, then it may be time to seek out some advice and support from trusted friends or family members.

Finding a partner who will help you move forward in life is important, but don't forget to take care of yourself along the way.

Importance in Healthy Boundaries with Self-esteem

Having healthy boundaries with self-esteem is key to a healthy relationship. When both partners understand what they want and expect from each other, they can have clear boundaries without compromising themselves or their partner.

Healthy boundaries with self-esteem are not only about basic needs such as sex, but it also includes other personal needs such as financial security or the need for space and independence. Intimacy with a partner is important but finding ways for both people to have autonomy in their relationship.

Healthy relationships with self-esteem can be built on honesty and communication with each other. Both people must be clear about what they want out of life, wants that are reasonable and achievable.

Many people are attracted to codependency, but they don't usually understand what they are attracted to. It is important to know what you want from a relationship before entering into one.

The following are some common misconceptions about codependency: a person with codependent tendencies can also become involved with other addictive behaviors such as alcohol or drugs. These individuals may find themselves in unhealthy relationships. In a healthy relationship, both partners can achieve their goals and live the lives they want without being dependent.

Avoiding problems and solving problems appropriately, instead of avoiding such issues and merely denying that they exist ("emotional avoidance"), can be a healthy way to deal with stress in relationships. When one partner fails to discuss a problem or express their feelings about something, this can create the feeling that there is some power struggle because they will not be heard.

To avoid those problems, it is very important for people who are emotionally dependent on others to do what they can to create healthy relationships. Problems must be discussed as soon as they appear and solutions suggested and implemented. Ideally, every situation should have a compromise solution that both partners can agree upon. It seems that we all want to be strong and fearless. I agree with these words, but if you think of the right meaning, I think it is more about overcoming any situation, not necessarily being strong physically.

Frequently the same words have different meanings when spoken to people from different backgrounds and cultures. Throughout my life and even today, certain words have different meanings depending on who I am talking to or what time of year it is. For example, in some cultures, "strong" means physical strength rather than mental strength when used by someone who does not follow that particular culture.

Chapter 16:
How Boundaries Affect Relationships

O ne of the challenges in relationships is setting boundaries to define each person's role. Boundaries give you a framework for your life and allow you to set limits on what you will do for others that might not directly benefit yourself or your loved one(s). Boundaries allow you to decide what you will put in (or on) and what will come out.

When these two principles are combined, boundaries become a way of life and not just something that exists within relationships. You can be completely social with people without any interest in having a relationship with you and know that you are not obligated to give them time or energy if they do not care for their part of the relationship.

Boundaries allow you to feel good about who you are and to truly enjoy (or end) a relationship on your terms. Unfortunately, many people struggle with knowing what their boundaries are within relationships. They may be afraid of letting the other person down or hurting someone's feelings if they set limits on what they are willing to do or give up for someone else. If we don't learn how to protect our time and energy, those things are taken by those around us unfairly.

Importance of Boundaries in Relationships

For many of us, setting boundaries in relationships comes naturally. It is important to understand that all relationships are different. Some people are used to putting up with things that others just don't realize they want. Other people may be more direct in their need for something (or someone) to stop doing things they do not want to do.

While boundaries may not be about how you and your loved one(s) communicate, it is one of the most important communication methods regardless of what type of relationship you have. If you do not teach your kids to communicate boundaries correctly in their relationships with others, they will learn this lesson the hard way.

When setting boundaries, you mustn't take on the burden of those who do not set boundaries for themselves. If your spouse does not respect your time and energy, it is up to them to set appropriate boundaries. However, you can allow them to rely on your help when they are unable to do so.

Healthy Relationships Always Have Boundaries

Healthy relationships always have boundaries. This is one of the biggest reasons why most of us like to keep our relationships healthy. Whether we are dating, married, in a relationship with family members or friends, or just interacting with those around us every day, our ability to communicate boundaries and how we feel about them is going to be instrumental in how we go about developing a positive relationship.

Learn to set boundaries for yourself, and those around you will begin to respect your opinions. Setting boundaries in relationships is one of the best ways to ensure that both parties involved have their needs met. This can be difficult for those who need to have things their way all of the time. This does not mean that you can't compromise or make concessions, but it does mean that the other person is important enough to be happy in a relationship.

Most of us are afraid at some point in our lives of having someone take advantage of us. If someone tries to cross your boundaries, you should be willing to stand up for yourself and let them know why this is unacceptable behavior and will not be tolerated. Those who set boundaries (or do not) will often find that it creates the type of relationship they desire.

Boundaries that Won't Work

Many people see boundaries as something that has to be "hard" to be effective. This is not the case. Boundaries that have to be hard and forced are counterproductive in learning how to set boundaries properly. Learning how to set boundaries in relationships can be difficult, but it can also lead to benefits for those around you and yourself.

When trying to understand how you can set better boundaries, you understand what doesn't work first. By doing this, you develop an idea of what will help make your boundaries stronger and better reflect what they need to do for the relationship at hand. How to go about it. It involves:

224

Controlling behavior: While you may have good intentions, trying to control another person's behavior is a sure way to create a negative relationship. Relationships are meant to be about cooperation in most cases. Having one partner try to force the other into doing something they do not want results in resentment and sometimes even further problems down the road.

Telling: Trying to tell someone what they have done wrong is not effective at creating boundaries in relationships. If you want your loved one(s) to understand what you are doing with your boundaries, explain them instead of telling them what needs to change within the relationship.

Being hostile: Being hostile towards your loved ones can lead to resentment, anger, and much worse than if you simply communicated what you needed from them.

Going away: Going away can easily set deeper limits on how far a relationship can go into the future. This is often difficult to do when one person feels like they cannot handle another person's behavior. This can also create resentment.

Chapter 17:
Respecting Other People's Boundaries

D on't take others' kindness for granted. We all have our limits, and they're not always easy to talk about. Respecting boundaries can make the world a better place. It can help you build relationships with those around you and foster an understanding of what's important. It can also keep you out of trouble.

Your limits are yours alone to set, and it's up to you how to communicate them. You have the right to ask for what you need in relationships and to let others know when they've crossed your boundaries. It's also possible that someone won't respect your boundaries, either because they didn't realize they'd crossed a line or because they don't care. If that happens, find someone who will listen and help you find ways to express your needs more clearly and have others respect those limits more fully in the future.

Boundaries are physical, emotional, verbal, and sexual. Examples of physical boundaries would be saying no to a hug or a kiss. Emotional boundaries can be things like setting aside time to meditate every day or doing special things yourself once in a while. Verbal boundaries might include telling others you will not discuss politics at work or that you don't want to hear their problems right now. Sexual boundaries can involve saying no to sexual activities where you don't feel safe or comfortable.

Focus on respect. A person's boundaries may not be the same as yours, but you can still show respect for them by respecting their feelings, values, and opinions. You have to listen carefully to how others express themselves. Keep your own needs under control. When we want something from others, it can be tempting to ignore or derail their attempts to communicate their boundaries. To respect someone's boundaries, let them communicate those boundaries and in a way that makes sense to them. If they need extra time or notice before making important decisions, give it to them. If they don't like hugging when they greet someone, don't force the hug. Avoid manipulation and coercion.

Be a good listener. Listen more than you say. Figure out what your partner wants and needs from you so that you know how to respond appropriately. Try to get in touch with feelings like sadness or anger and share them with your partner without judging or criticizing their response. Ultimately, you want to create an environment where your partner feels safe and free to address anything without feeling judged.

Listen for verbal cues. People sometimes have a hard time talking about their boundaries, but they may still communicate with them. Listening for verbal and nonverbal cues can help you understand when someone is uncomfortable with something you are doing. If you hear a "yes" that sounds hesitant, notice a lack of eye contact, or see fidgeting, pay attention to those clues. It's also important to know that those who engage in sex for money or survival (prostitutes/sex workers) often use code words to keep themselves safe. So if someone says they are "working" or "not feeling well" instead of saying no, it doesn't always mean yes.

In the end, the ultimate goal of respecting other people's boundaries is to help you build a healthy relationship. If you have a hard time respecting others' boundary, try to put yourself in their shoes and think about what would be most helpful for them. If you need support, find someone who can help you sort out your feelings and needs. There are many resources available online (see below) and local support services that can help you learn how to communicate your needs and feelings more effectively. Respect yourself.

Pay attention to body language. We can't always hear what other people are saying, but we can often read their expressions. If your partner is uncomfortable with something you are asking for or doing, you should stop doing it until your partner agrees to crossing the boundary. For example, if someone says no to having a hug from you, don't ignore them and wait until they say yes because that can leave them feeling trapped and uncomfortable.

Set clear limits in advance. Sometimes people have blocked areas of their lives that make it hard for them to communicate boundaries. Dating people and negotiating sex can be tough, so both people should set clear boundaries before beginning any sexual activity. This can help keep people safe and free from unwanted consequences later on.

Get respectful. If you are interested in getting a little more risqué with your partner who seems reluctant, consider asking them what they need to feel more comfortable. Whatever you do, make sure that you respect their wishes and follow through on what you say. Don't talk about one thing but then do another or say one thing but mean another because it will lead to problems, especially if the other person feels they can't speak up for themselves.

Know when things have changed. Some things that you have agreed to do in the past might not be okay anymore. For example, suppose the two of you have talked about intercourse, and it kissing was only done when you were dating. It might not be okay to have sex until after your relationship has become more serious. Communicate clearly so that both people know where everyone stands.

Communication is Key

Another way to make sure good relationships are created has good communication skills with your partner(s). This skill is very important as it helps define your boundaries and how far you want them to go. Communication enables you to grow as a couple by discussing what each partner wants and needs. Communication is not the same as talking. It is an art form that requires more than just verbal communication; it also involves nonverbal communication.

Communication is one of the most important skills you can have as an individual or couple, and it's what makes good relationships great. Good communicators are better listeners, negotiators, and problem solvers. It's no wonder that good communication skills are associated with healthier relationships.

Good communication also means that everyone involved in the relationship has input into decision-making processes or events. Communication can also be how you get your needs met and express yourself about important issues.

Communication is the key to a healthy relationship. You need it to manage conflict, make decisions together, solve problems, have fun, and even just be friends! Communication is how people exchange ideas, information, or feelings using spoken or written words. The goal of communication is not just to have a conversation; it's about sharing things to create relationships. Both verbal and nonverbal communication is needed for a relationship to be successful.

Chapter 18:
Exploring Relationships Gone Wrong

I n relationships, the key is always to be a good person who's trying their best. Relationships are not one-sided; they are reciprocal. You must both work on the relationship for it to last and stay happy. When you're working on your relationship, you have something to talk about and learn from each other; when you stop working on your relationship, that's when things go wrong.

What does this mean exactly? It means that as soon as one person stops trying for the relationship - even if it's just a little bit - everything changes. Suddenly there is less conversation, less connection, less understanding of how the other person works and lives.

In a healthier relationship, you're both working on it. You are both trying to be understanding of each other and make sure the other person is happy. When this stops, there is an enormous loss concerning communication, one that can potentially destroy a relationship.

In a relationship gone wrong, there is an imbalance of power. One person is trying to do everything possible to hold the relationship together, while the other person has given up. How does this look?

Relationship gone wrong

A girl is doing all she can to hold on to what little she has, while her boyfriend is content with letting her go and no longer working at it. One person does all they can to keep the relationship going, while the other does nothing but let it fall apart. There are definite stages that a relationship goes through when it's going bad. They are as follows:

1. Everything is fine, but you notice something has changed. The other person seems more irritable, more distant, or even sometimes happy for no real reason. The phrase most commonly characterizes this stage as "something's different."

2. You confront the problem, and the other person says they're just having a bad day and won't happen again. The other person usually acts as nothing happened, and this stage is often characterized by the phrase, "It's gonna be okay."

3. You confront the problem again, and this time, the other person loses their temper. They yell and scream and curse you out. This stage is characterized by phrases such as, "You never understand," or "Can't you just leave me alone?"

4. You walk away from the confrontation because you're tired of dealing with it, but the cold truth is that this stage has already claimed your relationship, and things will never be okay again. This stage is characterized by phrases such as, "This isn't working anymore," or "It's over."

Notice how each phrase falls into a category? There's something different on Day 1, a confrontation on Day 2, a fight on Day 3, and finally acceptance on Day 4.

These stages can happen within minutes, hours, or even days of the initial problem. It's all up to the other person. In my experience, Day 4 is inevitable so long as you allow it to happen; but sometimes it never even gets to that point, and the relationship ends by itself. Either way, if you allow problems in your relationships to go unresolved for long periods, you allow them to overtake you and destroy your relationship from within.

Remember: when one person stops trying for the relationship, everything changes, including YOU!

How Does Lack Work on a Relationship Cause Damage?

Your similarities begin to feel less like they are something you have in common and more like a way to judge the other person for being different from time to time. As the relationship starts to stop working, you start to criticize them for things that didn't use to matter: their taste in music, their choice of clothing, or even how they do something they're good at. Instead of discussing these things and then maybe finding out what they mean for both of you as a couple, you ignore them and let them go.

In time, the other person stops caring about these things - or worse yet, they resent you for not caring enough so they could spend more time talking about it. A lack of work on a relationship causes more damage than the actual fights themselves. There is a constant cycle of one fight that stops working and then another fight for no good reason. People see you as having a bad relationship from the outside, but you're just fighting and bickering over nothing from the inside.

The thing is, if you stop fighting altogether, there won't be any negativity. There will be an understanding - and even love - that wants to exist in your relationship despite what things seem like from the outside. It will feel like everything is fine; both you and your partner will want to stay together and be happy to try whatever it takes to make it work.

Take the Relationship Back From the Brink

If you notice that your relationship is not working, instead of freaking out or trying to fix it on your own without talking to your partner, the first thing is get in touch with them and talk about it. When you talk about it with your partner, there are a few things you can do.

Make sure that both of you understand how each other feels about the situation. If they give an answer that makes sense to both of you, then tell them that it's okay and that, ultimately, this is likely a misunderstanding. If you have an issue with something that they do or don't do, tell them how it makes you feel. This can be very empowering for both of you; but if things get out of control, be sure to listen as well as explain. Try to understand where they are coming from; and if you truly understand how they feel about a situation, then apologize for whatever may or may not have happened.

Ultimately it's up to both of you to work on your relationship so that it stays healthy and happy. If one person starts losing hope, then everything becomes ten times worse because the other person knows that one person is looking for a way out. It's hard to recover from this.

If you're in a relationship and this is happening to you, try not to focus on the negative. Instead, think about ways you can keep the relationship positive and happy for both of you!

How to Keep Relationships Healthy

The first step is to make sure that you are both working on the relationship. In any other kind of situation, this would never happen. But in relationships, it can - and it does. Start by talking less about issues that don't matter much to either of you; if something doesn't matter, why talk about it? Try talking with your other half about things that do matter.

Second, try using an online quiz or test together that reveals your strengths to help determine how the two of you work together and try your best to do more things together to utilize these strengths. The key takeaway here is this: the more you both do, the better it will be for you.

Conclusion

O kay, now take a deep breath. It seems like this is a lot of information to take in at once. You may be feeling several things. You could be motivated to go out and make changes right now. Hang onto that feeling and go forward. It's best to work while you're motivated so you can continue with your path to success. However, be sure to pace yourself so you don't burn out. If you start too fast, you'll run out of steam and end up giving up on your goal.

You might also be feeling overwhelmed by the information, by what you figured out about yourself, and by what you realize others have been doing to you. Understand that this feeling is only going to last for a moment.

Some of you may feel relieved and like you're not alone in that feeling. You may be relieved that there are changes you can make to alter your life right now. That relief you're feeling right now shows that you've been under stress and pressure. Use this relief to build your motivation to start saying no and standing up for yourself.

Now think to yourself what is the definition of a people pleaser. Do you think that includes you? Do you know someone who's a people pleaser? I think we can all agree that a people pleaser is someone willing to bend and fold for the opportunity to please others. Being a people pleaser can feel fulfilling; however, when done incorrectly, it can seriously cause harm for you and those around you.

Overall, you're going to want to do a couple of things to learn how to stop being a people pleaser. First, you're going to want to discover who you are. You can't properly help other people when you don't know yourself. When you know who you are, you're more confident. You're going to learn how to stop being so hard on yourself and find thhe unhealthy behaviors that upset you and then fix them.

Next, you're going to address any negative experiences, trauma, or insecurities you might have. Reach into the deep, dark parts of yourself and find the real reason behind your thoughts and actions. You're going to work on your lack of self-esteem and your ability to be so impressionable by the people around you. You want to be the one who leaves an impression on others.

Moving forward, you'll set boundaries for yourself and your life. These boundaries are going to protect you from hurting or harming yourself. These boundaries are also going to keep those around you safe from being hurt by you. When you set boundaries, you're taking part in self-compassion. Make your boundaries and learn how to stick with them.

Next, you're going to say, no. That's right. Now you can say, no. Not only because you know how to say, no, but you trust yourself more to say it. You've got all this knowledge and confidence, so you can be certain that you can start saying, no. It may even be unconscious... for some of you, this may be easier than for others. But one sure thing is that everyone can do it.

Don't forget to stay strong. At this point, you've probably created ways of staying strong. Throughout the reading of this book, you've probably paused and thought to yourself what you would I do if I were in a certain situation. This is you creating coping mechanisms. When you create a plan to stay strong, make sure you include these mechanisms. They can get you over the hard times when you can't reach out to your support team. Stay strong when handling your reactions. They can go one way or the other, good or bad. Regardless of the outcome, you have to trust yourself and stick to what you say.

Always remember to express yourself. Expressing yourself is one of the biggest ways to build confidence. Expressing yourself is different for everyone, and that's the beauty of it. Whether you're expressing yourself through social interactions or activities, be aware that you're expressing yourself. Be happy at the moment that you're allowed to be you. After all, the brain changes for the better during self-expression.

Next, be assertive. Being passive gets you taken advantage of, and being aggressive gets you in trouble. Being assertive gets your point across in a confident, clear, and controlled manner. When you speak with logic and reason, people are more open to listen versus when you're screaming and speaking out of emotion. Be confident in what you're saying, don't leave any room for guessing, and control your tone and emotions when you're delivering your message.

Now that we're at the finish line, it is time to make a game plan. Once you do the needed changes within, you can perform your changes on the outside. It all starts with you and taking steps to a happier life. Sometimes those steps might include therapy, and that's okay.

Therapy can be helpful for most anyone and especially helpful for a person who is a severe people pleaser.

Last but not least, don't get upset. This may not work on the first try. You may use these behaviors for a week and then resort to your old ways. One, you will get tired of what you're going through and blow up. It will take a hard, abrupt realization for you to make the changes you need in your life.

You are going to start saying, no. You're going to start practicing tomorrow! You will take it and run with it and make the best of it that you can. Change is a different pace for everyone; it's not a race.

Reforming yourself as a people pleaser is a journey, not a destination. This isn't saying that you're never going to say, yes, again without regretting it. But now you know what harm it can do, you can better control when you say, no. Now you can determine when you want to set boundaries.